THE CAR IS ARCHITECTURE
A Visual History of **Frank Lloyd Wright's** *85 Cars and One Motorcycle*

RICHIE HERINK

Fideli Publishing Inc.
119 W. Morgan St.
Martinsville, IN
46151

© Copyright 2015, Richie Herink

All Rights Reserved.

No part of this book may be reproduced, stored in a retrieval system, or transmitted by any means, electronic, mechanical, photocopying, recording, or otherwise, without written permission from the author.

ISBN: 978-1-60414-843-5

The author has made every attempt to locate the copyright owner for the cutaway drawing of the Mercedes-Benz 300SL without success.

The cover photo of Wright's modified 1940 Lincoln Continental convertible was taken by Thomas A. Heinz.

The picture of the Lincoln, Cord, and AC in a lineup on page 98 was taken by Charles Richardson.

The American Austin, Bantam News cover on page 48 was produced by Bob and Cathy Cunningham.

The photo of the Crosley Hot Shot on page 21 was taken by Dr. Joe Rorke.

The photo on page 13 was taken by Ron Kimball.

The magazine and newspaper ads were edited by Don Manza.

Copies of *The Car Is Architecture* are available at quantity discounts from the publisher.

CONTENTS and CHRONOLOGY

PREFACE vii

THE WRIGHT CARS: AN OVERVIEW 1

GETTING THE WRIGHT CARS RIGHT 15

1867 Frank Lloyd Wright was born on 6/8/1867

A VISUAL HISTORY OF THE WRIGHT CARS 23

Year acquired/model year

1909 STODDARD-DAYTON, roadster, rented from C.W. Vail 24

1911 KNOX, roadster, first car Wright owned 25

1912 CADILLAC, phaeton, first electric self-starter 26

1917 OVERLAND, Country Club, roadster 27

1920/1919 CADILLAC, phaeton, type 57, purchased used 28

1921 CADILLAC, type 59, purchased for Aisaku Hayashi, Japan 29

1923 CADILLAC, type 61, designed by Harley Earl, purchased used 30

1927 "Frank Lloyd Wright Inc." beginning of FLW brand

1928 DODGE, Victory 6, brougham, purchased 2 cars 31

1928 FORD, Model A, phaeton 32

1929 DODGE, Victory 6, with CANTRELL wood body 33

1929/1925 PACKARD, Model 8, phaeton, 244, purchased used 34

1929 CORD, L-29, 4-door convertible 35

1932 FLW Fellowship started

1933 Taliesin to Taliesin West to Taliesin treks begin

1934 FORD, club cabriolet 36

1935 Cherokee Red, Duco color, adopted by FLW

1935 FORD, convertible sedan, special extended trunk................................37

1935 FORD, station wagon...38

1935 FORD, convertible coupe...39

1936 FORD, convertible sedan 40

1936 FORD, station wagon, purchased 2 cars..41

1936 LINCOLN ZEPHYR, 2-door sedan 42

1936 LINCOLN ZEPHYR, 2-door coupe..43

1937 Wright stopped driving at age 70

1937 FORD, station wagon..44

1938 MERCURY, convertible coupe..45

1939 BANTAM, roadster, 2-passenger...46

1939 BANTAM, speedster, 4-passenger, purchased 3 cars 47

1939 BANTAM, station wagon...48

1939 BANTAM, pickup truck 49

1939 BANTAM, Speedster and station wagon...49

1939 BANTAM, panel truck 50

1939 LINCOLN ZEPHYR, convertible coupe..51

1939 LINCOLN CONTINENTAL, convertible coupe 52

1940 Frank Lloyd Wright Foundation formed

1941 LINCOLN CONTINENTAL, 2-door sedan 53

1942 WWII, civilian automobile production stops

1942 LINCOLN CONTINENTAL, convertible remodeling proposal

1943/1930 HARLEY-DAVIDSON, motorcycle, model #30VL............................ 54

1945 WWII ends, automobile production resumes

1946 WILLYS, 'JEEP,' CJ2A, civilian Jeep 55

1946 WILLYS, 'JEEP' station wagon 56

1948 WILLYS 'JEEP,' CJ2A, civilian Jeep 57

1948 CROSLEY, pickup truck 58

1948/1937 AC, Ace, 16/80, sports car, purchased used 59

1948 JAGUAR, Mark IV, 2-door convertible, spare tire on trunk 60

1948 Wright's 1940 LINCOLN CONTINENTAL, convertible, customized 61

1949 JAGUAR, Mark V, 4-door sedan 62

1949 CROSLEY, Hotshot roadster, purchased 2 cars 63

1949 CROSLEY, station wagon 64

1950 Cherokee Red #2, red shade NASH, car color first appearance

1950 CROSLEY, Hotshot roadster, purchased 3 cars 65

1950 CROSLEY, Super station wagon, purchased 2 cars 66

1951 CROSLEY, station wagon 67

1951 CROSLEY, Farm-O-Road, dual rear wheels 68

1951 RILEY, RMB, 4-door sedan 69

1952 MG-TD, 2-passenger sports car 70

1952 AUSTIN, Somerset, A40, 4-door sedan 71

1952 CROSLEY, Supersport, purchased 6 cars 72

1952 HILLMAN MINX, convertible, 3-way top, purchased 3 cars 73

1952 HILLMAN MINX, 4-door sedan, purchased 3 cars 74

1952/1929 CORD, L-29, 2-door Cabriolet, purchased used 75

1953 FORD, Victoria, 2-door hardtop 76

1953 FORD, Country Squire, station wagon 77

v

1953 FORD, Ranch Wagon, 2-door, station wagon... 78
1953 PONTIAC, Catalina, 2-door, hardtop 79
1953 CHEVROLET, Carryall, Suburban, station wagon... 80
1953 JAGUAR, Mark VII, 4-door sedan, automatic 81
1953 LAND ROVER, Series 1, purchased used 82
1955 ROAD MACHINE, Broad Acre City vehicle proposal viii
1955 CHEVROLET, Nomad, station wagon 83
1955 MERCEDES BENZ, 220A, 4-door sedan... 84
1956 MERCEDES BENZ, 300SL, gull-wing sports car 85
1956 MERCEDES BENZ, 300C, 4-door sedan... 86
1956 PONTIAC, 4-door sedan 87
1956 VOLKSWAGEN, Beetle 88
1956 VOLKSWAGEN, Karmann Ghia, engine replaced 1958 89
1956 VOLKSWAGEN, Kombie... 90
1956 VOLKSWAGEN, Pickup.. 91
1958/1953 BENTLEY, James Young, Sedanca, purchased used............................ 92
1958 PANHARD, Dyna, 4-door sedan 93
1958 PLYMOUTH, Fury, apprentices' gift to Olgivanna, FLW's wife 94
1958 SEARS, Lectracar, golf cart, gift from H. Price 95
1959 PONTIAC, 4-door sedan, purchased for Iovanna, FLW's daughter................ 96
1959 (Frank Lloyd Wright died on April 9, 1959 at age 91)

APPENDIX

Final Inventory of Frank Lloyd Wright Foundation cars.. 97
Wright's Car-Related Projects.. 99
Acknowledgements 101

"The car is architecture."
—Frank Lloyd Wright

PREFACE

This historic publication brings to light the little known fact that the automobile was one of Frank Lloyd Wright's passions and that buying cars was one of his obsessions.

Wright, through his Frank Lloyd Wright Foundation, owned more cars and more different makes and models of cars than any other architect that ever lived.

Wright purchased cars even when he was financially strapped and he often bought several cars at once. Nearly all of his cars were painted Cherokee red, regardless of their original factory color. The first Cherokee red was a dark maroon color used by the 1935 Oldsmobile. The second version was a shade of Wisconsin barn red that was used by the 1950 Nash Rambler. Incidentally, this car was also manufactured in Wisconsin.

Wright, thereby, turned his cars into Frank Lloyd Wright cars, irrespective of their make and model. It was part of the way he established "Frank Lloyd Wright" as a brand name and he used his automobiles to draw attention to himself and to provide him with the outward appearance of success.

This is a visual history of the one motorcycle and the 85 cars that Frank Lloyd Wright purchased or rented throughout his lifetime.

Because photos of only a few of his cars are available, historic magazine ads that depict, in their illustrations, the year, make, and model of each of his cars are used to describe them, thereby providing, in effect, a history of these cars as told via the automobile manufacturers' own magazine advertising.

This book answers the following questions: How many cars did Frank Lloyd Wright own? What were their makes and models? And, what did they look like?

The Car is Architecture

After five years of on and off research, I believe that I have accurately identified all of Frank Lloyd Wright's cars. However, it is possible that one or two additional makes and models could surface once researchers are allowed access to the restricted documents in the Frank Lloyd Wright Foundation's own archives at Taliesin West in Scottsdale, Arizona. Unfortunately, two of the identifications contained herein are not on solid ground — the 1912 Cadillac and the custom built Cadillac that Wright described in his autobiography. The others are well documented by information from written primary sources.

Frank Lloyd Wright was famous as America's greatest architect. But he was original in another way you never suspected. Here's his design for your 1960 car

THE WRIGHT CARS

AN OVERVIEW

Frank Lloyd Wright was born in 1867, two years after the American Civil War ended. At the time, the modes of personal land transportation consisted of walking, horseback riding, the use of horse drawn vehicles of various types, including carriages, stagecoaches, and streetcars, plus railroad trains which began to blanket the United States. There were almost no paved roads and travel was very time-consuming and subject to the tyranny of railroad and bus time schedules and the weather.

From 1899 to 1911, when Wright lived in Oak Park, Illinois, a suburb of Chicago, with his wife and their six children, he commuted by train to Chicago where he worked as an architect.

The first American car was built in 1893 by the two Duryea brothers in Springfield, Massachusetts. Wright was 26 years old at that time. It was basically a horse-drawn buckboard without a horse. The engine was mounted under the front bench-type seat and it drove the rear wheels. A boat tiller was used for steering the front wheels. It was, as its nickname implied, a "horseless carriage."

In 1900, the first front engine cars appeared with the engine located under a hood. This was the beginning of the automobile having a distinctive look of its own.

On February 17, 1906, *Oak Leaves,* the local newspaper, published a survey that showed that there were 82 cars registered in Oak Park, of which four were manufactured by Stoddard-Dayton. It also stated that Oak Park boasted of having "the greatest number of autos of any community its size in the country."

In 1909, at age 42, Frank Lloyd Wright obtained his first car. It was a Stoddard-Dayton roadster with a single rumble seat in the back. The car was painted yellow, a factory option. Wright either rented or borrowed the car from Charley Vail, who lived in Chicago. This answers the often asked questions of: Where did Wright get the money to buy the car and what happened to it when he left for Europe? Mr. Vail owned it.

In 1909, there were 123,990 cars sold in the United States, consisting of 290 different makes produced in 145 cities in 24 states. A Stoddard-Dayton won the first Indianapolis Speedway race, which was run in 1909.

According to Wright's son, John, in his book, *My Father Frank Lloyd Wright,* "The good citizens of Oak Park (Illinois) called it the Yellow Devil, and not many days passed before the Oak Park police department threatened to confiscate it" because of the excessive speed at which he and his father drove the car around town. If Wright wanted attention, he certainly got it with this very visible yellow automobile.

In October of 1908, the Ford Motor Company launched the Model-T Ford at a price of $850. This car became "the car that put the world on wheels." By the end of its production run in 1926, the price of the Model-T was reduced to $350, made possible by continuously improving production efficiencies. Henry Ford was realizing his dream of "empowering the masses" by providing them with cheap, reliable transportation. In 1926, Ford was building Model-T cars and trucks at the rate of 9,000 units per day in the United States alone. By the mid-1920s, half of the cars in the world were Model-T Fords.

Since that time, many architects, including Frank Lloyd Wright, dreamed of emulating Henry Ford by being able to manufacture low cost houses on an assembly line as cheaply as Ford built vehicles.

Frank Lloyd Wright's 1911 to 1917 American Readi-Cut System of prefabricated homes was an unsuccessful step in this direction. He was apparently more interested in designing kits than in their assembly.

In 1909, Henry Ford hired Frank Lloyd Wright to design a Prairie School-style house for his Fair Lane estate in Dearborn, Michigan. Soon after Wright started working on its design, he left his wife and children and ran off to Europe with

Mamah Borthwick Cheney, a married woman with two children who also lived in Oak Park. Wright assigned his talented employee, Marion Mahony, to complete the Ford job.

It was during this early phase of their home's design that Henry Ford and his wife Clara traveled on vacation to Europe, where they became enamored with the architecture of European mansions. Upon their return, they dismissed Mahony and Wright, and brought in architect William Van Tine to redesign the house by giving it an English manor look. Wright never worked for Henry Ford again.

Yet, in spite of being fired by Henry Ford, during his lifetime Wright purchased 19 Ford Motor Company-built Ford, Lincoln and Mercury cars. They ranged from one of the first Model-A Fords in 1928 to a Ford Victoria hardtop and two Ford station wagons in 1953.

Frank Lloyd Wright's best known car was a Ford product — a Cherokee red painted, 1940 Lincoln Continental convertible. Its look was modified in 1948 by the Ideal Body Company in Madison, Wisconsin and involved a redesign of the upper body that consisted of cut down windshield and door glass, plus the installation of a permanent Sedanca Coupé-type half-roof with half-round side windows and no rear window. Wright claimed that he did not need a rear window because he never looked back. Then again, he stopped driving in 1937 and had no reason to. (Ideal is still in business at the same location with the son of the original owner running the business.)

In 1911, Wright purchased his first car. It was a Knox roadster with two rumble seats in the back and a side-mounted spare tire. The July 22, 1911 issue of *Oak Leaves,* the Oak Park newspaper, stated, "Frank Lloyd Wright is suffering from a broken arm, caused by the crank of his automobile which struck him when the engine started."

In his book, *An Autobiography,* Wright discusses his accident as follows: "Due to a compound fracture of the wrist I got while cranking the heavy Knox roadster I owned (after the Stoddard-Dayton), I kept a driver at Oak Park for a time. He was very careful of my broken member — but eventually stole the car. He turned out to be one of a gang of auto thieves. The police finally got the car in a St. Louis barn as they were putting a coat of green paint over the gunmetal finish… I never cared for the Knox anyway, at high speed it would settle down and shake itself almost to pieces in a perfect frenzy. (The garage doctors call it a shimmy. And they could not show it how not to.)"

The second car Wright purchased appears to be a 1912 Cadillac touring car. There is only anecdotal evidence of its existence. However, given Wright's experience with crank-starting the Knox, it is reasonable to assume that his next car would be the only car available at the time with an electric self-starter, the 1912 Cadillac — "the car without a crank."

Besides the 1912 Cadillac, the other car that was difficult to pin down was the Cadillac that Wright mentioned in his book, *An Autobiography*. This is how he described it: "I think I got the most enjoyment (1922, '23, '24) out of the long, low, black specially built Cadillac as out of the Cord. Patent leather Victoria hood over the rear seat, windshield between the front and back seat, no footboards, sides built down. I drove it in L.A. when I returned from Japan. That Cadillac thus had the look of the later Cord—streamlined, very compact. Wherever we parked, the crowd would gather to see the 'foreign car' — trying to guess the make." Note: It is not clear that Wright actually lived in Los Angeles in 1922.

The one car that best fits this description happens to be a custom designed Type 61 Cadillac, with a Victoria top, that was styled by Harley Earl before he joined General Motors. It may have been originally built by Don Lee's Coach and Body works in Los Angeles for the film and stage actress Ann May. Wright apparently purchased it when he opened an office in Los Angeles in 1923.

These and all of Frank Lloyd Wright's other cars are depicted elsewhere in this publication.

Over his lifetime, Frank Lloyd Wright purchased, on behalf of either himself or the Frank Lloyd Wright Foundation, the following car makes, with the number of cars for each make shown in parenthesis when the number exceeds one.

They are: AC, Austin, Bantam (7), Bentley, Cadillac (4), Chevrolet (2), Cord (2), Crosley (17), Dodge (3), Ford (13), Hillman-Minx (6), Jaguar (3), Jeep (2), Knox,

Land Rover, Lincoln (5), Mercedes Benz (3), Mercury, MG-TD, Overland, Packard, Panhard, Pontiac (3), Riley, Volkswagen (4), and a Willys.

In all, Wright purchased 85 cars from 1911 to 1959, the year he died. The last car he bought was a 1959 Pontiac for his daughter, Iovanna. In 1960, his wife Olgivanna purchased a 1960 Pontiac for herself, which was paid for by the Frank Lloyd Wright Foundation.

In addition, Wright purchased one Harley-Davidson motorcycle and two small, Bantam-built enclosed car trailers. In 1958, he received one Sears Lectracar golf cart as a gift from Harold Price, and Olgivanna received a Plymouth Fury as a gift from two apprentices, Kay and Davy Davidson. Not included are Wright's trucks, farm equipment and one authentic stagecoach.

Wright also prepared sketches of two unique cars and a mobile kitchen, none of which were built. In 1942, he proposed a remodeling of his 1940 Lincoln Continental convertible, which provided the inspiration for the 1948 customization of his car after it had been involved in an accident in Iowa in 1946. These items have not been included in this publication due to royalty costs and other related reasons.

Over his lifetime Wright purchased more makes and models of cars than any other architect to date.

While Frank Lloyd Wright was witnessing the development of the automobile into an increasingly effective mode of individualized transportation, he also saw it become the greatest agent for social, economic, environmental, and personal change that the world has ever known. America had become a car-culture nation almost overnight and became a country whose people were always on the go traveling somewhere by car — to stores, work, movies, restaurants, visiting family and friends, running errands, seeing clients, taking children to school, etc.

In her article, "General Motors Innovations in Class Structure," Katherine Mechler observed, "In the early years of the automobile industry, Henry Ford created a mass-produced automobile at declining cost, eliminating the car as merely a toy for the rich. An 'equality of conditions' was formed in which all had access to the automobile… Equality did not eliminate the need for individualism… Ford may have eliminated the status of car ownership, but he did not eliminate the status associated with owning a particular make and model."

After himself, Frank Lloyd Wright's next great passion was architecture in all of its manifestations. Next came Japanese art and third, automobiles. In a speech before the Michigan Society of Architects in Detroit on October 21, 1957, Wright described architecture in the following broad terms: "There isn't anything connected with your lives that isn't architecture. Your clothes, the way you dress, the way you live, the way you sit down and eat and what you eat. The car is architecture."

Wright's fascination with the automobile is further illustrated by remarks made by two of the very limited groups of people who knew him best of all. In her 1959 book, *Our House,* his third wife, Olgivanna, stated: "Some of our apprentices are at first shocked that the discussions held in the dining room at mealtime are: moving pictures; second, foreign cars; and third in line, and very sparingly, architecture."

Bruce Brooks Pfieffer, former director of the Frank Lloyd Wright Archives and author of numerous books about Wright, stated in his book *Treasures at Taliesin,* "Wright loved automobiles. In fact, they were one of his passions. Regardless of his personal finances, he always drove marvelous cars. ... In Paris in 1956, he saw the new model of the Citroen Palos DS 19, which was not available for export at the time. He admired its design and the engineering, and if he could have, he would have taken one home with him."

If the car is architecture, then Wright's association with the automobile should be made part of his life's story. Not only did the automobile provide Wright with on-demand mobility, it also provided him with a new source of potential business opportunities.

Over the years, Wright prepared numerous car-oriented architectural design proposals including the following: an "automobile objective and planetarium" in 1924; a roadside filling station in 1931; a standardized gas station in 1932; a highway overpass in 1934; a service station/restaurant in 1943; a butterfly wing-shaped bridge in 1947; a drive-in national bank and an automobile sales/service dealership in 1947; a San Francisco bridge and a self-service parking garage in 1949; a "paradise on wheels" housing project in 1952; a Jaguar showroom in 1954; a motel in 1956; a gas station in 1956; two motels in 1957; and in 1932 with a revision in 1958 the master plan for an entire city called Broad Acre that was tied together by the residents' use of a special car called a "road machine." A drawing of the car is shown on page viii.

Only two of these proposals were ever built: the 1956 Lindholm Phillips 66 gas station that is located in Cloquit, Minnesota (photo on page 100), and the 1954 Jaguar showroom in New York City that became a Mercedes-Benz showroom. It has recently been torn down. (Photo on page 99.)

Wright's New York challenge was to take a small, corner store that was part of a tall office building designed by Emory Roth Architects, located on fashionable Park Avenue, and turn it into an automobile showroom. Besides its small size, the space also had a structural building column in the middle of the floor. Wright tried a number of times to get the column moved — without success. So, he wrapped a floor-to-ceiling spiral ramp around it, with the ramp being the width of a car. He then installed a round turntable on the floor with the column as its center.

With automobiles parked on both the ramp and the rotating turntable, the visual effect was that of cars coming down from the ceiling onto the turntable in the form of an unintended "from heaven to earth" type of symbolism.

Next, Wright installed mirrors on every interior surface, including the structural column and its ramp, in order to make the showroom look much larger than it was. The result was the creation of an iconic automobile showroom for Mercedes-Benz in the middle of one of the largest cities in the world.

The showroom and the gas station represent the extent of Wright's contributions to America's car-culture that were actually built.

Wright claimed that he invented the carport, yet very few of his houses have carports or what could be called a type of carport. The first was the 1930s Jacobs House. There is no proof that his claim is valid. Variants of the porte-cochere had been around centuries before Wright was born.

In her book, *American Architecture and the Mechanics of Fame,* Roxanne Williamson stated: "Two of the most famous architects born in America were also the most active self-promoters in American architectural history." They were Louis Sullivan and Frank Lloyd Wright. She goes on to say, "Frank Lloyd Wright was a full participant in all aspects of self-promotion."

Not only was Frank Lloyd Wright a self-promoter, he was a *full-time* self-promoter. Without benefit of a public relations staff, he single-handedly maximized his visibility through his writings, lectures, exhibitions of his work, and, of course, via the advanced designs of his buildings. For a time, during his television appearances near the end of his career, he became "America's Architect" and its leading architectural critic.

Even the way he looked was attention getting. He wore a "pork pie" hat, put on extra clothing to look more substantial and carried a cane that he did not need but used to make a point when walking and carrying on a conversation. The use of his middle name also had an attention getting resonance — Frankie Wright vs. Frank Wright vs. Frank Lloyd Wright.

Perhaps his greatest invention of all was himself and he spent nearly all of his life being Frank Lloyd Wright. Even today, Frank Lloyd Wright is better known to the general public than most of the presidents of the United States, even the more recent ones.

The automobile also played a role in helping Wright enhance his image. He bought or rented up-scale cars for his and his wife's use. They included the Stoddard-Dayton, the Knox, the Cadillacs, an L-29 Cord, a Packard, the Lincolns, the Jaguars, a Bentley and the Mercedes-Benzs. He purchased blue-collar cars such as Fords and Pontiacs for his staff and family, and unique, inexpensive, small cars like the Bantams, Crosleys and Hillmans for use primarily by his apprentices.

The first cars he owned were open-topped cars in which he could be seen sitting behind the steering wheel driving the car. After he stopped driving, at age 70, he was seen being driven in mostly closed cars, often riding in the front seat. This public visibility, plus his on-going new car purchases were outward displays of conspicuous consumption and success that he continuously engaged in even when he was broke.

While there were a number of famous industrial designers who drove highly customized cars for personal and professional visibility, including Raymond Loewy,

Albrecht Goetz, and Brooks Stevens, Wright appears to be the only architect to take full advantage of the car's innate ability to attract attention to its owner. Not only did he own a customized Lincoln Continental but he also painted all of his cars in the same distinctive shade of red. This is the same inexpensive brand identification technique that UPS uses today when they paint all of their delivery trucks in the same dark brown color and that Tiffany employs with its turquoise-colored shopping bags and gift boxes,

In 1935, Wright chose a dark burgundy Duco paint color called "Cherokee red" that was being offered by Oldsmobile at the time. In 1950, his new signature color became a 1951 Nash Rambler color called Pan American red. Note: the 1951 Rambler was introduced in the summer of 1950 and Nash used the color for only one year. It is similar to the color used on Wisconsin barns. Then again, the Rambler was manufactured in Kenosha, Wisconsin. Over time, in the Wright community, Pan American red evolved into being called Cherokee red, and at times Taliesin red.

There are, therefore, two different Cherokee reds — one used before World War II and the other used soon afterward. None of these colors are part of the Pantone ink color matching system, making it almost impossible to reproduce the exact colors in magazine articles and other printed literature.

Wright's credit must have been good because he never seemed to have difficulty getting financing for his cars. The exception was the 1929 Cord 4-door convertible, whose $400 per month payments nearly bankrupted him.

According to Julia Meech, author of the book *Frank Lloyd Wright and the Art of Japan,* "Wright's career as a dealer (in Asian Art) at one time rivaled his architectural practice in terms of both the attention that he devoted to it and his financial gain."

It is possible that some of the money from Wright's Asian art sales was used to pay for his cars. He coincidently purchased cars and sold art in: 1911 (Knox), 1912 (Cadillac), 1917 (Overland), late 1919 (Cadillac), 1922 (Cadillac), and in 1928 (Dodge and Ford). In addition, he was always trading in older cars for new ones. For example, a 1939 Lincoln Zephyr convertible was traded in for a 1940 Lincoln Continental convertible.

Despite being a car buff, Wright rarely spoke about his cars in public or in his books and writings. Wright's autobiography only mentions the Stoddard-Dayton, the Knox, the Cadillac with the Victoria top, the Cord phaeton, and a Packard sport phaeton. (Incidentally, a Victoria top looks like the hood on a baby carriage.) Then again, the public associated Frank Lloyd Wright with "modern architecture" and this was the subject they wanted him to speak and write about.

There have been a number of magazine articles written about Wright's interest in cars. They include: "The Showroom that Wright Built" by Sam Posey, "The Wright Way" by Michael Jordan, "Frank Lloyd Wright — Automobility" by Steward Wells, "The Wright Stuff" by Steve Thompson, "Machines for Living" by Paul Goldberger, "Trekking to Usonia" by James Hockenhull, "Cross Country Caravan" and "The Glamour of the Red Convertible" by Ben Masselink, "Architecture and the Automobile" by Dixie Legler, "The Lincoln Continentals" by Dave Cole, "The Wright Bantams for the Job" by Cathy Cunningham, "A Tale of Two Cords: Frank Lloyd Wright's L-29 Phaeton and Cabriolet" and "Frank Lloyd Wright & His Automobiles" by Mary Jane Hamilton.

All of these articles put together barely scratch the surface of Wright's relationship with the automobile. In addition, a number of them contain factual errors, which are discussed in the chapter "Getting the Wright Cars Right."

It is evident that in order to complete the Frank Lloyd Wright story, his automania had to be documented. The following three basic questions, therefore, had to be answered: How many cars did he buy? What were their makes and models? And what did they look like?

At the time this research effort was first undertaken in the summer of 2005, Mary Jane Hamilton and Rachel Corey had independently done research at the Frank Lloyd Wright Archives in Scottsdale, Arizona for material needed to write articles about different aspects of Wright's car ownership. Ms. Hamilton's focus was on Wright's L-29 Cords and Ms. Corey had to discontinue her efforts documenting Wright's small cars because of schedule constraints. Neither was working on a total inventory.

Both authors were contacted and these are their observations about the problems associated with researching Wright's cars. Rachel Corey stated, "No one kept track of the cars. A lot of people who know what happened to his cars or worked on his cars or drove with him (Wright) are getting older and perhaps are not even living anymore. "The records were not kept, they were ignored, and were either being thrown away or disintegrating… Cars are mentioned in passing in accounts of apprentices who paid no attention to his cars (even though they were driving them or sitting in them for hours on end)."

Mary Jane Hamilton cautioned, "If your proposed list of cars is to be considered definitive, I believe you are in for a long search for dated correspondence and photos. My experience with the two L-29 Cords was enough to show me that not much information is out there. I hope you can do the homework needed to come up with a truly comprehensive list that can be confirmed with conclusive documentation."

In other words, what the two researchers were saying was do not take anything that was written or being said about Wright's cars at face value and do not expect to receive a lot of cooperation from the Wright apprentices, since many were not around when Wright was alive. So, a decision was made to use source documents and expertise whenever possible for the identification of Wright's cars.

Naturally, the first place to look for original reference material was the Frank Lloyd Wright Archives located at that time in his Taliesin West facility in Scottsdale, Arizona, which contained Wright's 103,000-document correspondence files in hard copy and on microfilm, plus 40,000 photographs, and the Frank Lloyd Wright Foundation's own business records. Since the Foundation owned nearly all of Wright's cars, this was the most logical and important place to start. In 2014, the Archives were moved to Columbia University in New York City.

Unfortunately, access to the Foundation's own records and the photographs was repeatedly denied. Only the microfilmed correspondence file was made available for research.

The J. Paul Getty Museum in Santa Monica, California also has a copy of the microfilmed correspondence file. Since it had reproduction capability and Taliesin West did not, The Getty was, therefore, used for the research.

Anthony Alofsin's book, *Frank Lloyd Wright: An Index to the Taliesin Correspondence,* Volume 5, was used to locate any and all correspondence that had the name of an automobile or an automobile-related firm listed on any mail going to or coming from Wright.

In addition, an unexpected source of information about Wright's cars came from Arnold Roy, an Arizona architect and former Wright apprentice. He provided an inventory of the cars and trucks that the Foundation owned at the time of Wright's death, which was taken for estate purposes.

The inventory identified several of Wright's cars that did not have any archival correspondence associated with them. They were: four Volkswagens, a Chevrolet Suburban, an Austin Somerset, two of the Pontiacs, and an electric golf cart.

Unfortunately, the list contained a few dating errors. The AC was acquired in 1948 not 1937, the Austin was a 1952 model not a 1951, the L-29 Cord two-door was acquired in 1952 not 1930, and the VW Karmann Ghia was obtained in 1956 not 1958. Its engine was replaced in 1958.

Since most of the documented information about Wright's cars is limited to year, make, and model, it was decided to present the inventory in a photo album format and to include a copy of an actual magazine ad for each car as part of its description. The result is a visual history of Frank Lloyd Wright's cars that uses advertising media to tell each car's story.

The magazine ads were obtained from eBay, dealers in automotive literature, garage sales, car clubs, the Antique Automobile Club of America's library, the Internet, and various car magazines.

Most difficult and time-consuming was acquiring ads of cars that looked just like Wright's cars except for their paint color.

Despite all of the obstacles encountered during the research process, Wright's passion for the automobile has been successfully proven by the identification of the sizable number and variety of cars he purchased during his lifetime.

When he died in 1959, Frank Lloyd Wright had been witness to the very beginning of the American automobile industry and the development of the automobile into a product of enormous utility and social relevance, with an artistic beauty of its own. And, he fully participated, as an owner and a driver, in its evolution from the early horseless carriage era to the striking tail fin designs of the 1950s — at which time large American cars began to look more like airplanes.

For a car enthusiast like Wright, life could not have been more interesting than this.

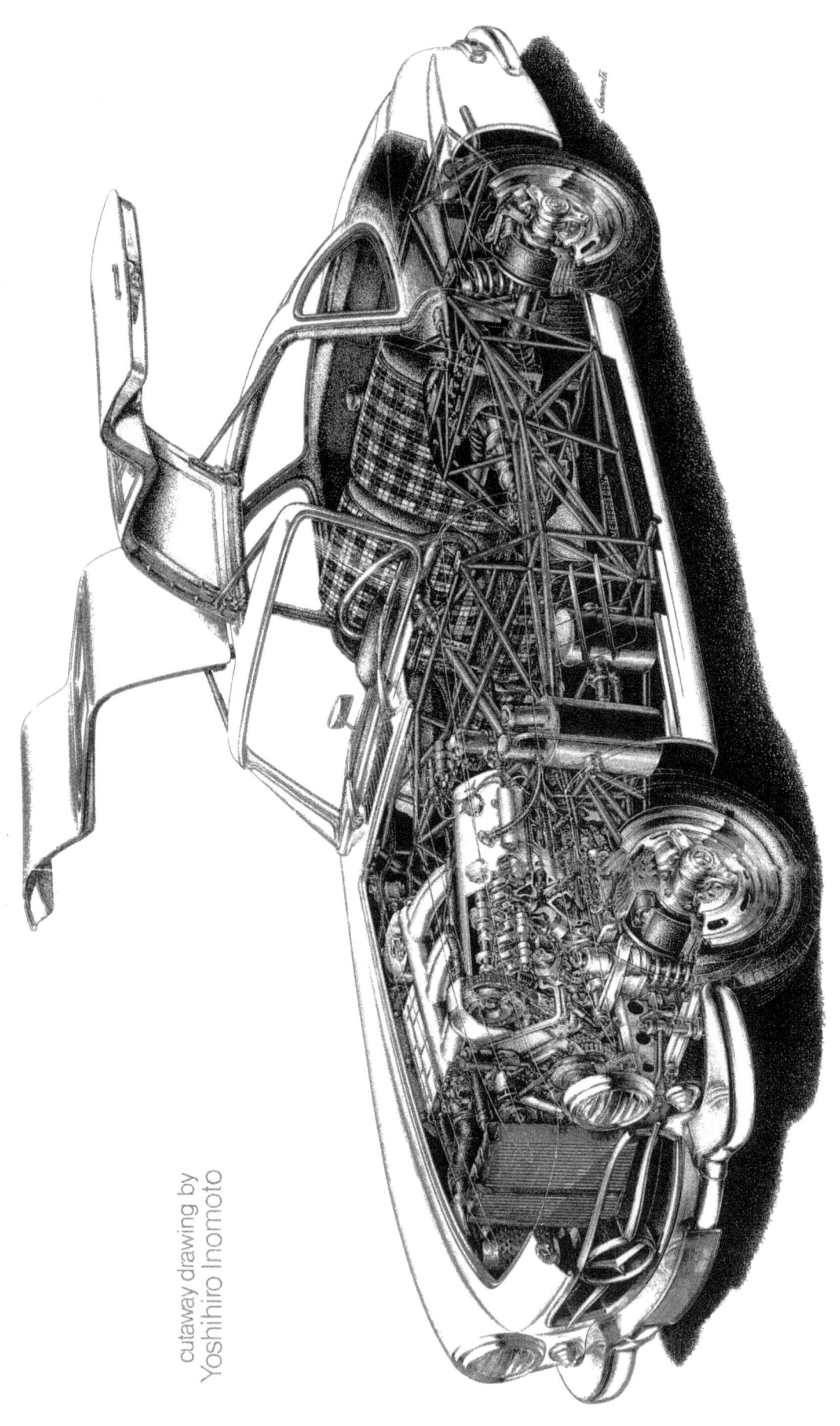

cutaway drawing by Yoshihiro Inomoto

GETTING THE WRIGHT CARS RIGHT

Given the variety and number of cars that Wright was involved with over a 50 year period, and the limited amount of car-related reference material that is available in the various Frank Lloyd Wright archives and collections, it is not surprising that a few misconceptions about his cars have entered the Wright literature.

This section addresses in more detail the most prevalent of them — starting with the origin of the Cherokee red paint color.

Perhaps the most common source of the origin of Cherokee red comes from Donald Hoffmann's book *Frank Lloyd Wright's Fallingwater*, which was published in 1978. The following quote is from the book:

Claim: "Mosher was also concerned about painting the steel sash and the other metal details ... Wright specified Duco, which Mosher thought could not be applied with a brush, although advertisements in the 1920s showed it being hand painted onto furniture. Wright asked the Du Pont Company of Wilmington, Delaware to mix the paint to a Cherokee red. He sent along an Indian pot as a color guide."

Response: In a letter dated May 10, 1935 to W.E. Simons of the Ford Motor Company branch in Milwaukee, Eugene Masselink, Wright's assistant, wrote the following: "On our return from Milwaukee yesterday we passed by the Oldsmobile garage and saw in the front of their salesroom a roadster with exactly the color that Wright wants for his convertible Ford sedan.

"I'm enclosing a sample. It is Duco paint #108 RM 20585. Will you please get this same paint for use on the car ... The trade name for the paint is Cherokee red."

The 1951 Nash Rambler Pan American red paint color was the successor to the original Cherokee red.

Wright did use another red color to paint the Mercedes-Benz 300SL and the bottom half of the body of his Mercedes-Benz 300C sedan whose roof, hood, trunk and fenders were painted black to create a two-tone effect. The red color was specially mixed at the factory for Wright. It is called "Brick Red #554." Unfortunately Mercedes-Benz lost the mixing formula.

According to John Setchell, the Advanced Color Technology Manager at Pantone, the printing ink manufacturer, there are no Pantone colors that correspond to any of these three reds or even come close. Therefore, the reds that you see in the photographs are really not the actual Wright colors.

Authentic paint chips for the Oldsmobile and Nash Rambler colors are still available from vendors at car shows or from Walter Miller in Syracuse, New York.

Note: The two restored Wright Lincoln Continentals that are owned by Joel Silver are not painted in either version of Cherokee red. The same is true for Wright's L29 Cord and the Crosley Hot Shot exhibited in the ACD Automobile Museum.

1925 Packard, Model 8, Phaeton

Wright purchased the Packard as a used car in May 1929 from the Packard Phoenix Motor Company in Phoenix, Arizona for $1,217. The car ended up having serious engine problems. It was replaced by the 1929 Cord L29 four-door convertible in November or December of 1929.

Claim: The caption of the photo of Wright's car in the 1996 Library of Congress exhibit; "Frank Lloyd Wright, Designs for an American Landscape," identifies the car as being a Cadillac.

Response: The car pictured was Wright's 1925 Packard. (A 1925 Packard is shown on page 34.)

1940, 1941 Lincoln Continentals

Claim: In her book *Frank Lloyd Wright,* Meryl Secrest reported: "Masselink recalled that when the first Lincoln Continentals appeared in 1937, he was invited on a trip to Chicago with Wright and his brother. They were driving down Michigan Avenue when Wright commanded them to stop in front of a Lincoln Continental dealership ... Mr. Wright went up to the new Lincoln, tapped on the fender with his cane and said, 'I want one of these and one of these. Gene, show him the color we want, the Cherokee red.' The salesman explained that the color would have to be a special order. Mr. Wright continued, 'I want a convertible top. Take that thing off. I will send you my own design — something like a roll top desk' ... Then he declared, 'and I don't intend to pay for them.'"

Response: In 1940 Wright purchased a Lincoln Continental convertible for himself and the following year, when it came out, the 1941 Lincoln Continental coupe for his wife, Olgivanna. Both cars were purchased from Monart Motors in Milwaukee. The convertible's purchase order was dated January 11, 1940.

Claim #2: A variant of the Secrest story can be found in the book *The Fellowship* by Roger Frieland and Harold Zellman. They state: "As a promotion, the Ford Motor Company had offered to give away a number of new models to prominent Americans, including Wright. When the architect appeared at the Chicago showroom, however, he demanded two — one for each of his estates ... Ford complied."

Response: Wright paid $3,195.50 for the Lincoln Continental convertible, according to the bill of sale previously cited. The price included $100.00 to have the car painted Cherokee red at the factory. The purchase order for the coupe is not available.

1940 Lincoln Continental Convertible's Customization

Claim: In the winter 1991 issue of the magazine *IL Quadrifoglio*, in an article titled "The Wright Lincoln Continental," the author Mark Burrell stated: "Within two years of its life at Taliesin, the Continental went upside down. One legend has it that Wright's daughter, Iovanna, wrecked it but (John) Hall remembers that it was Wright's son-in-law, Wesley Peters. Wright sketched preliminary designs for the new car. The Ideal Body Shop in Madison built the components, rear top and windshield."

Response: Indira Berndtson, a member of the Frank Lloyd Wright Foundation, in a November 11, 1998 unsent letter to Michael Jordan, a writer for *Automobile* magazine, stated: "In 1994, I interviewed Ted Bower, an apprentice from 1941-1948, who told me that he had been driving the car when the accident occurred which subsequently caused Frank Lloyd Wright to remodel it. I also interviewed two of the passengers in the car at the time — Irene and Noni Buitenkant, who confirmed Mr. Bower's information that they were traveling together from Taliesin West to Taliesin in Wisconsin and the accident happened in Iowa, circa 1946."

It appears that after the 1946 accident, the Lincoln Continental convertible was shipped to Coachcraft Ltd. in Hollywood, California for its repair and body customization. Coachcraft was a well-known designer and builder of custom cars for movie stars and other celebrities. They were particularly known for their Sedanca tops, which were similar to the one that Wright wanted for his car. These half tops are also called coupe de ville or cabriolet tops.

In a letter dated February 12, 1947, Coachcraft gave Wright an estimate of $1,800-$2,000 to repair the car and to build and install a metal Sedanca top and modify the vehicle's windshield and side windows. Wright declined the offer.

The car was then shipped or driven to the Walker Body Works in nearby Los Angeles where it was repaired back to its original working condition. The repairs included: removing and replacing both doors, repairing the right rear fender, removing and repairing the radiator, straightening the hood, repainting the car, etc. For all of this work Wright paid $204.50. This work was completed on May 10, 1947.

Sometime later, the car was driven or shipped to Wisconsin where the Ideal Body Shop in Madison did the customization at a presumably much lower price than what Coachcraft was asking for.

In a letter dated August 31, 1948, addressed to the Arizona Vehicle Division, Masselink states the following: "Enclosed please find 1947 Arizona Title and Registration for Lincoln Continental 1940 Convertible Cabriolet. This car has not been driven for the past year following an accident. Repairs are nearly complete and we want to bring the title up to date."

The letter was sent from Taliesin in Spring Green, Wisconsin, thereby completing the story of the customization of the Lincoln Continental convertible.

1956 Mercedes-Benz 300C Sedan and 300SL Sports Car

Claim: Frank Lloyd Wright traded his commission for designing Max Hoffman's Jaguar/Mercedes-Benz automobile showroom on New York's Park Avenue and his house in Rye, New York for the above two Mercedes-Benz vehicles.

Response: Frank Lloyd Wright Archives document #H164810 references purchase contract #19357 and #19538 for the two Mercedes-Benz cars. It requests $7,566.80 as balance of the purchase price of both cars.

Note: There is no documentation that states that Wright received any car or cars in exchange for his design services and this includes the two 1928 Dodge Victory 6 Broughams in exchange for his work on the Biltmore Hotel in Scottsdale, Arizona

However, in a letter dated July 14, 1952 to Max Hoffman, Wright stated: "If this does not disturb your wish to have me design your country home — all right — we will take delivery of the two Porsche cars and pay the balance due, what ever it is."

Wright wanted one Porsche convertible and one Porsche hard top. Hoffman turned down Wright's offer.

1909 Stoddard-Dayton

Claim: Everyone believed that Frank Lloyd Wright owned a Stoddard-Dayton automobile, even members of his family. In his book *My Father Who Art On Earth,* John Lloyd Wright described the arrival of the Stoddard-Dayton as follows: "Excitement ran high. The four-cylinder, three-seater Stoddard-Dayton sport roadster arrived. It was one of three automobiles in all of Oak Park. Dad had the factory remake their original body according to his own design ... The trimmings were brass, the body enameled straw yellow..."

Response: As we now know, John's statement is not at all true. The car belonged to Charley Vail and there were at least 61 cars in Oak Park at the beginning of 1906.

The unanswered question is: Why did Charlie Vail, a Chicago politician, rent or loan the car to Wright after he had just bought it, and why did he sell it after Wright left for Europe instead of keeping it for himself? There is no record in the Illinois Automobile License files that shows Vail owning any car in 1910, 1911 or 1912, or previously in 1907 or 1908.

The model type of the Stoddard-Dayton is unknown. Since neither Wright nor Vail were men of means, it is most likely that Vail purchased the least expensive model — the 9H Runabout, which listed for $1,525. This was an era in which the median price for a new home was around $3,000 and median yearly salary was under $600.

Incidentally, on April 5, 2006, Casie Kesterson, a Getty Museum researcher, told me that a 1909 vehicle registration tag that was found in the basement of Frank Lloyd Wright's Oak Park home, was being auctioned on eBay. I bid $50 and it sold for $500. Nevertheless, the information on the tag turned out to be almost priceless in its ability to shed light on the real story of the Stoddard-Dayton, namely that Wright never owned the car.

The other unanswered questions are: How did the tag get into Wright's basement and when did it get there?

Other Comments: There are also misconceptions that involve car ownership including, for example, the 1948 Jaguar Mark IV and the 1956 Mercedes-Benz 300SL were owned by the Frank Lloyd Wright Foundation and not by Wes Peters.

There is no available documented evidence that Wright ever bought or received, during his lifetime, any of the following cars: Cord model 810/812, Duesenberg, Morgan, Rolls Royce or any other makes not listed in this publication.

The Crosley Hot Shot shown below was assembled from two junkable cars by a local mechanic after Wright died in 1959. One car was a 1952 model and it is registered accordingly. It is not part of this inventory. It can be seen at the ACD Automobile Museum. The photo below shows the car with a group of student apprentices at Taliesin West.

TODAY AS YESTERDAY — **1909 STODDARD-DAYTON** was typical of its day and proved quite popular. Priced at $2,500, it offered a four-cylinder, 36-horsepower engine. It was manufactured in Dayton, Ohio.

Cars run their best on the best gasoline

1916 OWEN was called "The Car of a Thousand Speeds." Its electromagnetic transmission anticipated today's automatic shifts.

1953 STUDEBAKER Starliner reflects European style in its low silhouette—less than five feet high. Power steering and a choice of transmissions are offered.

1933 LEVER claimed "50% saving in fuel...100 miles per hour" because of its trick engine. A lever linkage between pistons and connecting rods was designed to increase torque at low engine speeds.

"ETHYL" (TRADE-MARK) ANTIKNOCK COMPOUND

ETHYL CORPORATION

New York 17, New York
Ethyl Antiknock Ltd., in Canada

Early-day automobile manufacturers often devised fantastic stunts to publicize their cars. One promoter actually hung a car and driver from a huge balloon and sent them sailing over Indianapolis, Indiana.

Probably he was trying to prove that his car had "high" performance. However, today's car owners have their feet on the ground when it comes to their cars' power and performance. And millions of them have found the way to get the best out of a modern high compression engine is by using "Ethyl" gasoline.

Next time you need gasoline, look for the "Ethyl" emblem. You'll enjoy the powerful difference between gasoline and "Ethyl" gasoline!

A VISUAL HISTORY OF THE WRIGHT CARS

If the car is architecture, then the cars Wright owned over his lifetime are an undocumented, yet integral part of his professional mystique. And just like Taliesin, Taliesin West, his original Oak Park house and their furnishings, they are an integral part of the architecture he owned and used.

The following section is a visual history of his car purchases. They are listed in chronological order, starting with Wright's first car, the 1909 Stoddard-Dayton roadster, which was either rented or borrowed from C.W. Vail.

All of the accompanying manufacturers' magazine and newspaper ads feature cars that look exactly like the cars that Wright purchased.

1909 STODDARD-DAYTON, roadster, rented from C.W. Vail

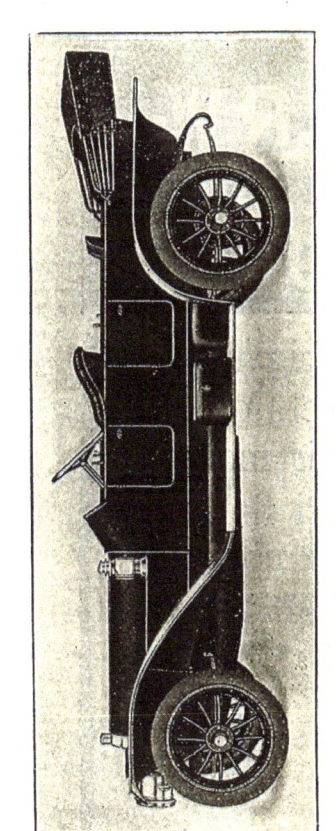
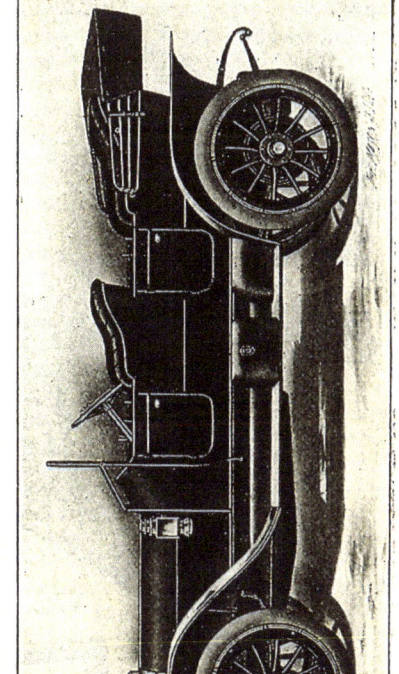
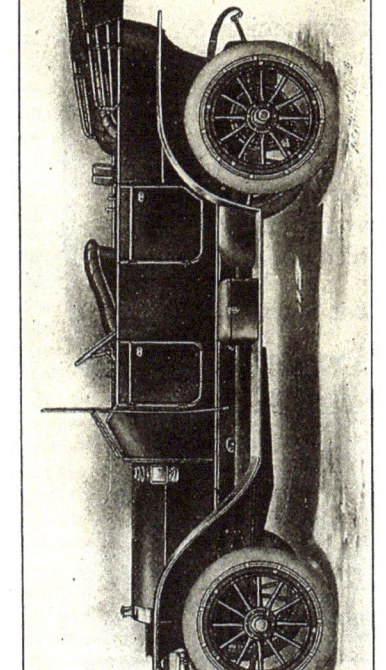
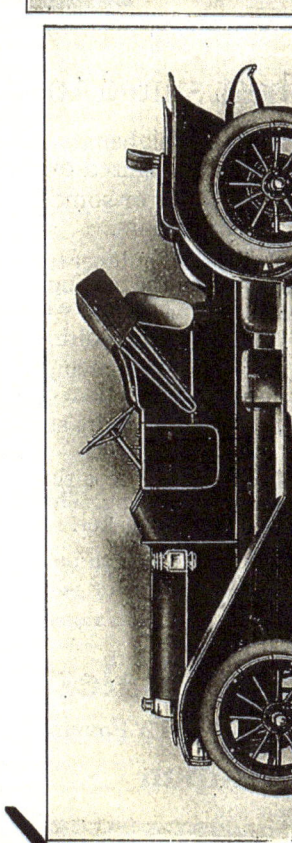

1911   ANNOUNCEMENT   1911
FOUR CYLINDER, 40 H.P.   SIX CYLINDER, 60 H.P.

STANDARD AND TORPEDO TYPE TOURING CARS, 5 and 7 passengers.
CLOSE COUPLED TYPES, LIMOUSINES AND LANDAULETS, made with detachable front seat doors.
TONNEAUETTES with Torpedo type front, high doors, made with tonneau detachable.
RACEABOUTS, made with or without Torpedo front and high doors.
TORPEDO TYPES, 4 and 6 passengers; the most beautiful cars of this type on the market.

KNOX TYPES OR FEATURES OF CONSTRUCTION ARE ORIGINAL NOT COPIES
SEND FOR ADVANCE INFORMATION

KNOX AUTOMOBILE COMPANY, Springfield, Mass.

1911 KNOX, roadster, first car Wright owned

The real value of the

is not adequately expressed by its price

If you are familiar with motor car conditions you know that the Cadillac dealer is practically outside the zone of competition.

Almost everybody is Cadillac-convinced—almost everybody concedes its unique reputation.

But have you realized the full and splendid extent of that reputation?

It was brought home to us (for the thousandth time) in a new way, the other day, when we banteringly asked one of the most prominent dealers in the Cadillac organization:

"Don't your customers *ever* speak of other cars in comparison with the Cadillac?"

And he answered in all seriousness: "Only those of the very highest price—*and then not in disparagement of the Cadillac.*"

Conditions in your own locality will confirm this.

And you can probably recall several instances—as nearly everyone can—in which the ownership of much higher priced cars has been exchanged for Cadillac ownership.

Taken together, the two sets of facts constitute a profession of confidence in the integrity of Cadillac construction which should be conclusive in establishing its value to you.

You know what a dependable car the Cadillac is. You will appreciate, therefore, how much it means when we say that there are now more than five thousand 1912 Cadillacs in the hands of more than five thousand enthusiastic users, who without exception are every day having demonstrated to them that the Delco system of automatic electric starting and electric lighting is precisely as dependable as every other feature of the Cadillac car.

Intensified by the luxury of the system which performs the triple function of starting, lighting and igniting, the *Perfectedness* of the Cadillac has reached a point which is not adequately expressed by the money cost of the car in comparison with existing price standards.

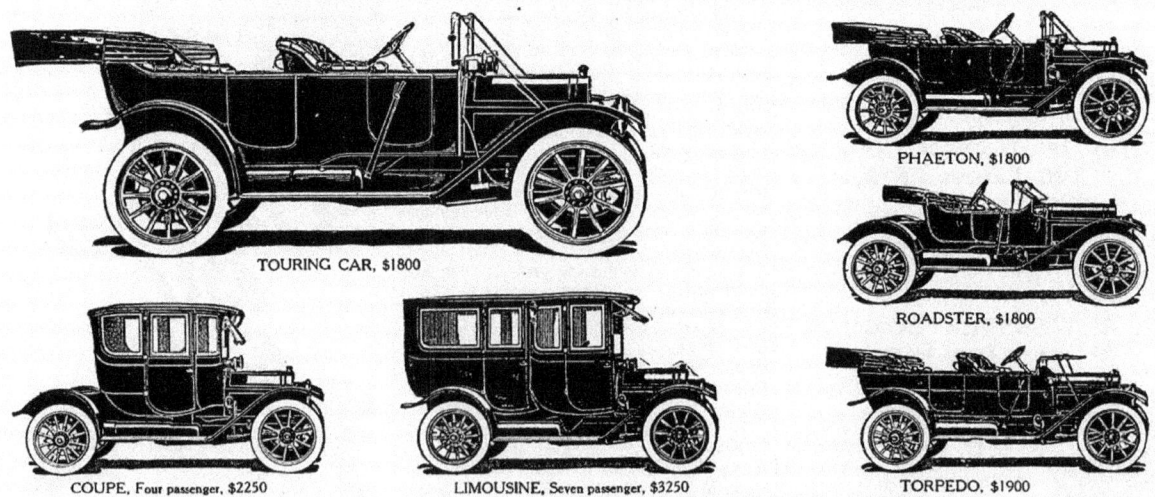

Prices are F. O. B. Detroit, and include standard equipment.

CADILLAC MOTOR CAR CO.   DETROIT, MICH.

1912 CADILLAC, phaeton, first electric self-starter

1917 OVERLAND, Country Club, roadster

1919 CADILLAC, phaeton, type 57, purchased used

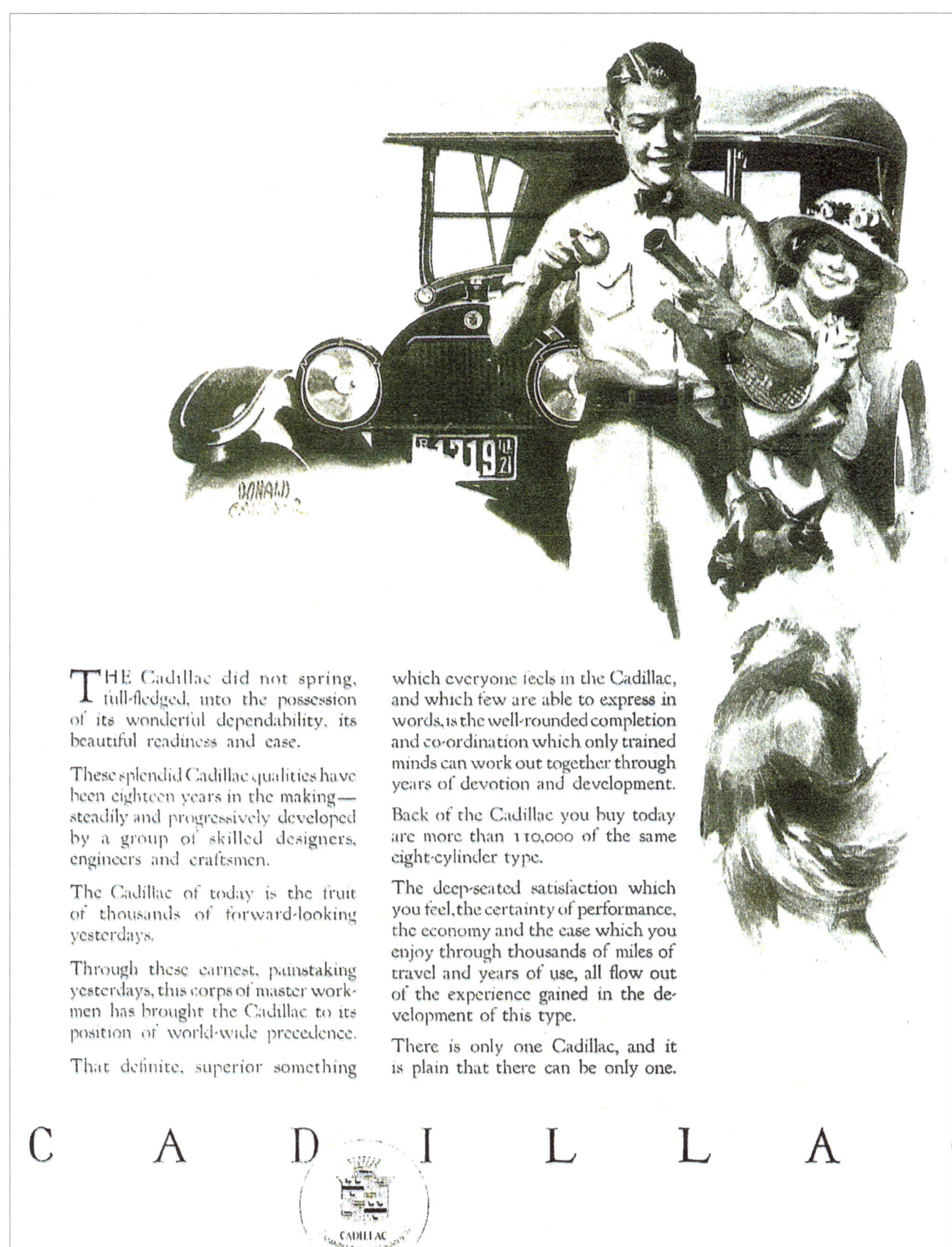

THE Cadillac did not spring, full-fledged, into the possession of its wonderful dependability, its beautiful readiness and ease.

These splendid Cadillac qualities have been eighteen years in the making — steadily and progressively developed by a group of skilled designers, engineers and craftsmen.

The Cadillac of today is the fruit of thousands of forward-looking yesterdays.

Through these earnest, painstaking yesterdays, this corps of master workmen has brought the Cadillac to its position of world-wide precedence.

That definite, superior something which everyone feels in the Cadillac, and which few are able to express in words, is the well-rounded completion and co-ordination which only trained minds can work out together through years of devotion and development.

Back of the Cadillac you buy today are more than 110,000 of the same eight-cylinder type.

The deep-seated satisfaction which you feel, the certainty of performance, the economy and the ease which you enjoy through thousands of miles of travel and years of use, all flow out of the experience gained in the development of this type.

There is only one Cadillac, and it is plain that there can be only one.

C A D I L L A

1921 CADILLAC, type 59, for Aisaku Hayashi, Japan

1923 CADILLAC, type 61, Harley Earl designed, purchased used

1928 DODGE, Victory 6, brougham (2 cars)

The Ford Phaeton

Features of the Ford car

Sturdy body construction ⊹ ⊹ Mechanical reliability ⊹ ⊹ Unusual number of ball and roller bearings ⊹ ⊹ Alemite chassis lubrication ⊹ ⊹ Choice of colors ⊹ ⊹ Four Houdaille hydraulic double-acting shock absorbers ⊹ ⊹ Triplex shatter-proof glass windshield ⊹ ⊹ Fully enclosed, silent six-brake system ⊹ ⊹ Quick acceleration ⊹ ⊹ 55 to 65 miles an hour ⊹ ⊹ Smoothness and security at all speeds ⊹ ⊹ Vibration-absorbing engine support ⊹ ⊹ Theft-proof ignition lock ⊹ ⊹ Economy and long life.

1928 FORD, Model A, phaeton

The Cantrell Suburban Body may be relied upon to give satisfaction under any conditions. Its many exclusive, patented features add to its refinement and increase its practicability.

This body can be supplied anywhere for the Dodge Standard Six and the Ford Chassis and, within driving distance of the factory, can also be supplied for the Buick, the Cadillac, and the Chrysler Chassis.

We shall be pleased to send you upon request our folder "C" giving details and specifications

J·T·CANTRELL & COMPANY
Makers of Suburban Bodies
HUNTINGTON, N.Y.

1929 DODGE, Victory 6, with CANTRELL wood body

Your 1925 Packard

Packard Six and Packard Eight both furnished in ten body types, open and enclosed. Packard's extremely liberal time-payment plan makes possible the immediate enjoyment of a Packard—purchasing out of income instead of capital.

The Packard you buy today will not look out of date in 1935

unless Packard is successful in doing

that which others have been unable to do —

improve on Packard lines.

If the industry, competing within itself, has been unable to improve on Packard lines

but rather, has appropriated them,

then, Packard has set an enduring style.

And, in an enduring style your motor car investment is best protected.

ASK THE MAN WHO OWNS ONE

1929 —1925 PACKARD, Model 8, phaeton, 244, purchased used

A new *kind* of motoring

It is very difficult to describe the exclusive advantages of the Cord without appearing to exaggerate. Everyone concedes however that nothing less than a totally new *kind* of motoring could make possible the successful invasion of the Cord into the fine car field. People accustomed to only the highest priced cars naturally assume they are enjoying the very utmost in transportation luxury. Some of them have told us about the cars they were driving: "It is difficult to conceive how my car could be improved;" "I am sure that nothing better could be built;" "I would not want anything finer."

Then they drove a Cord!

The more prejudiced they are, the more surprised they are when they learn the great difference in comfort, safety and driving ease that the Cord introduces.

Their former standards of comparison are immediately obsoleted. The contrast is so great that thousands of owners now tell us that their Cord cars spoil them for other cars. Once they have experienced the effortless handling, the different roadability, the sense of security, and the absence of fatigue, they are intolerant of anything less efficient and commodious.

It is self evident that the exclusive advantages resulting from front-drive construction are obtainable in no other way. Particularly is this true of its maneuverability, the way it holds the road, and the relaxation possible in the rear seat. If you have never ridden in the rear seat of a Cord we promise you a revelation. Select a route with which you are familiar, one over which you have ridden many times, and ride in the rear seat of a Cord over this route. We leave the verdict entirely to you. After such an experience you will be eager to learn more about this car, why it performs differently, why it "feels" different and why it gives you a renewed zest in motoring.

It is a matter of record that no new car was ever built with greater care, and with more extreme measures to insure its quality than were taken by the builders of the Cord. But our vigilance did not end with the Cord's introduction. Since then owners have been regularly canvassed for their opinions. A continuously improved car is the result.

Today the Cord is an even more efficient, an even more quiet, and an even more refined car than the ultra standard that it inaugurated.

SEDAN $3095 . . BROUGHAM $3095 . . CABRIOLET $3295 . . PHAETON $3295   Prices F. O. B. Auburn, Indiana. *Equipment other than standard, extra*
AUBURN AUTOMOBILE COMPANY · AUBURN, INDIANA

CORD FRONT DRIVE

1929 CORD, L-29, 4 door convertible

THE FORD V·8

THE FORD IS PART OF THE PICTURE

The alert, capable Ford V-8 is part of the picture of every activity. . . . For the gay, glad spirit of Youth is in it—an eagerness to be doing things and going places in a thoroughly modern manner. . . . You catch a suggestion of this as you watch the Fords go by—trim, lithe and colorful. You are very sure of it as you drive the car and note how swiftly, silently and comfortably you travel along. . . . Smooth power flows through quiet gears—the quick response of the car commands your confidence—you realize that it makes quite a difference when there's a V-8 cylinder engine under the hood. . . . Truly, a new thrill in motoring awaits you in the Ford V-8.

September 1934 Good Housekeeping

1934 FORD, club cabriolet

"Watch The Fords Go By"

MORE THAN two million Ford V-8's have been built. You see them everywhere, in city, town and country. V-8 has come to mean Ford.... Yet it has not been long since the V-8 car was only for the well-to-do. Its superior performance was recognized, but the price was high. You had to pay more than $2000.... So the Ford Motor Company set out to build a V-8 engine within reach of the average motorist.... That was something new and there were many who said it couldn't be done. But it meant better service to the public. Progress is always easier when you start with that idea.... Out of it came the Ford V-8—a wholly new kind of automobile for millions of drivers. Ford methods have made the full measure of performance, comfort, safety, beauty and convenience—once enjoyed only by the limited few—available to all at a low price. That is the meaning of the V-8 insignia.

1935 FORD, convertible sedan, special extended trunk

HAS SPEED, UTILITY AND ECONOMY

PANEL DELIVERY • This is a popular model in a wide variety of businesses, offering unusually large load space for units of this type. The hardwood floor is protected by steel skid-strips. Steel panels along the interior side walls extend to the tops of the wheel housings, and, from there up to the ceiling, the body is protected by hardwood slats. Load space same as the De Luxe Panel Delivery. Dome light is operated by a convenient switch in driver's compartment.

DE LUXE PANEL DELIVERY • Load space measures 77⅞ inches long, 51 inches wide and 51½ inches high. The interior is lined with heavy, insulating board. The rear view mirror and brackets are chromium plated as is the windshield wiper-blade holder. It is equipped with twin matched tone de luxe horns. These de luxe appointments reach a new high note of distinction in modern commercial car design. The wheels are enameled in colors that harmonize with body.

✓ **STATION WAGON** • Combines the facilities of a passenger car and a light hauling unit. This unit features de luxe passenger car appointments throughout. It carries seven passengers comfortably. The rear seats are quickly and easily removed providing space for carrying baggage. Safety glass is standard in front doors and windshield. The tailgate can be lowered and used as a luggage carrier.

SEDAN DELIVERY • The smartest shop can add to its prestige by displaying its name on the panel of this modern, good-looking, new delivery car. But its popularity is not limited to exclusive stores. Its price is so low it is a favorite in a wide range of businesses. The load space of the body measures 65 inches long, 44 inches high and 46¾ inches wide. Passenger car appointments. The interior is completely insulated. Wheels are enameled to harmonize with body color.

1935 FORD, station wagon

THE NEW FOUR-PASSENGER CLUB CABRIOLET

"Watch The Fords Go By"

Most often "it's a Ford" that steps out ahead at the traffic light. And does it so easily! No fuss or effort. Seems to just glide away in a smooth-flowing surge of power. . . . There's no surprise at this alert acceleration—you've come to expect it of a V-8. For many months, motorists have seen the Ford set the pace in traffic, on hills and on the open road. Frequently, you have heard it said—"The V-8 engine is the finest engine Ford has ever built." . . . Today's Ford gives you modern V-8 performance, with outstanding reliability and low cost. Its economy has been proved on the road by nearly three million Ford V-8 owners. . . . Each year the Ford brings you more in value—each year it costs less to run.

THE FORD V·8

1935 FORD, convertible coupe

V·8 Is The Mark Of The Modern Car

The Ford is an exceptionally good choice for the woman motorist because it is so dependable and easy to handle. That has always been so. These days there is still another reason for its ever-widening popularity—it is a thoroughly modern car. The Ford is as up-to-date in performance, comfort and safety as in appearance and appointment. Here are some modern features of the Ford... V-8 ENGINE (fine-car acceleration, power and smoothness—increased motoring enjoyment).... CENTER-POISE RIDING (greater comfort, front and rear—you ride near the center of the car instead of over the axles).... SAFETY GLASS all around at no additional cost (an important reason why the Ford is such a safe car to drive).... NEW STEEL WHEELS (distinctive design—large hub caps—big six-inch tires).... COMPLETE LINE OF BODIES (seventeen types, including new Convertible Sedan with trunk, illustrated above).... It's altogether modern, this alert, spirited Ford V-8—in a class by itself because of many exclusive features.

FORD V·8 FOR 1936

$25 A MONTH, WITH USUAL DOWN-PAYMENT, BUYS ANY NEW FORD V-8 CAR ON NEW UCC ½ PER CENT PER MONTH FINANCE PLANS

Good Housekeeping	May, 1936	Better Homes and Gardens	May, 1936	Liberty	May 2, 1936	Collier's . . . . . May 16, 1936
Ladies' Home Journal	May, 1936	McCall's	May, 1936	Time	May 4, 1936	Farmer's Wife . . . June, 1936
Woman's Home Companion	May, 1936	Vogue	May 1, 1936	The Saturday Evening Post	May 23, 1936	Household Magazine . June, 1936
		Holland's Magazine		June, 1936		

1936 FORD, convertible sedan

PANEL DELIVERY

A good-looking delivery unit for the merchant whose loads range between those cared for by the 131½-inch Panel and the Sedan Delivery. Load space is 82 inches long at floor, 51 inches wide and 51½ inches high. Door opening is 42 inches wide by 44⅛ inches high. Doors are dust-proofed and are equipped with an independent lock.

DE LUXE PANEL DELIVERY

Same load space and door opening as Panel Delivery. De Luxe equipment includes interior lined with heavy insulating material, twin matched-tone de luxe horns, chromium-plated windshield wiper blade holder and chromium-plated rear vision mirror. Big 6.00 x 16 tires on 4-inch rims standard on all commercial car models.

STATION WAGON

Combines facilities of a passenger car with those of a light commercial unit. Seats 7 passengers comfortably. Rear seats can be removed, providing load space. Tailgate equipped with compensating spring. Features De Luxe passenger car appointments. Safety Glass in two front doors and in windshield.

SEDAN DELIVERY

A full-sized delivery unit on the regular 112-inch wheelbase. Design follows closely that of 1936 Ford V-8 passenger cars. Load space is 65 inches long at the floor, 46¾ inches wide and 44 inches high . . . an unusual amount of load space for this type of unit. Four shock absorbers and Safety Glass throughout standard at no extra cost.

1936 FORD, station wagon (2 cars)

1936 LINCOLN ZEPHYR, 2-door sedan

1936 LINCOLN ZEPHYR, 2-door coupe

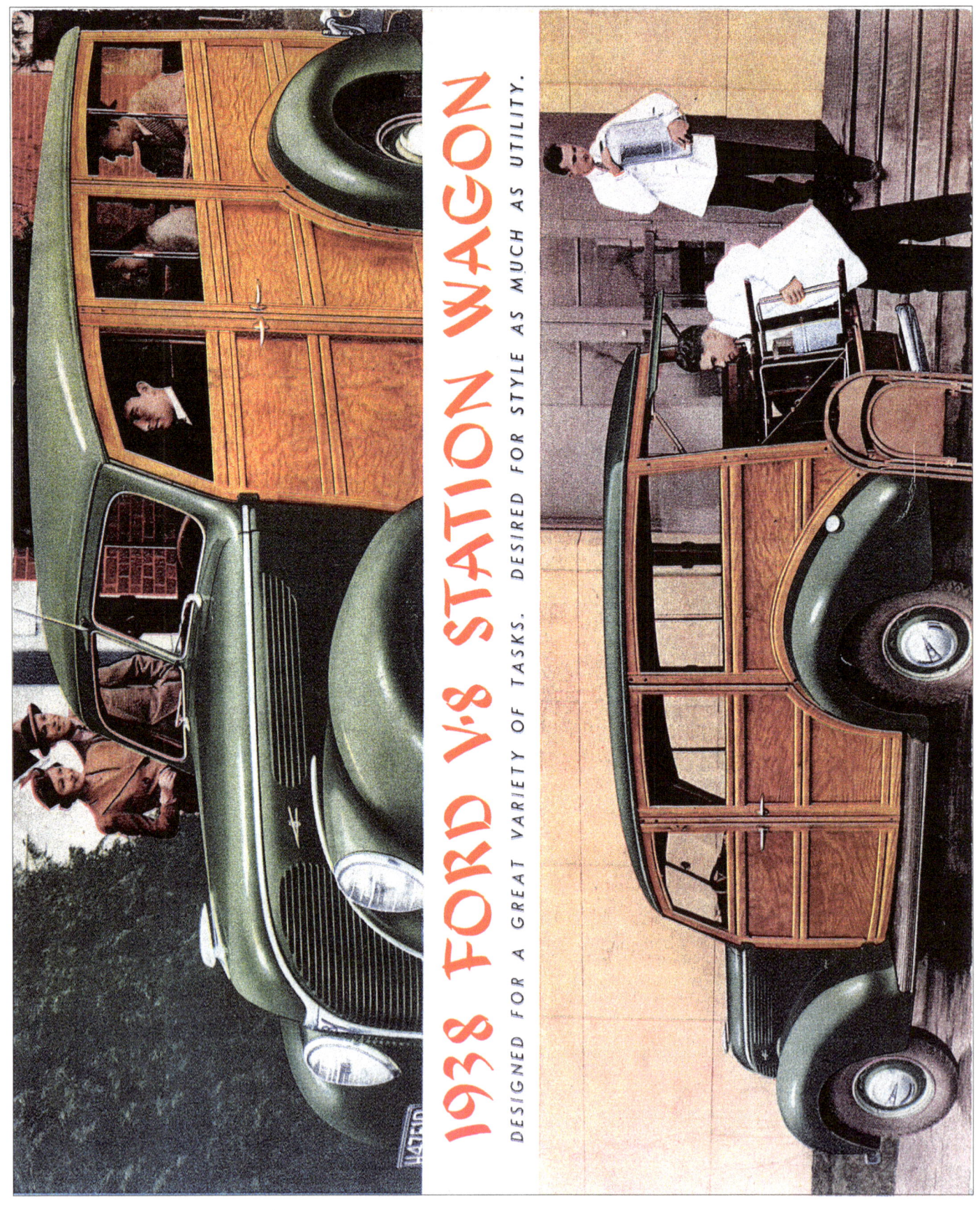

1937 FORD, station wagon

Thirty-five years ago, the Ford Motor Company manufactured its first automobile. The accumulated experience of all those years now finds new expression in the Mercury 8 . . . designed to extend Ford-Lincoln standards of mechanical excellence, progressive design and outstanding value to a new price field.

THE NEW MERCURY 8
A PRODUCT OF THE FORD MOTOR COMPANY

There's something as new as the Spring in the clean, sweeping lines of the Mercury 8. It is wide and remarkably roomy, but skilful design has made its bulk beautiful. • There's extra smoothness and silence, too, as well as extra space. Soundproofing materials help reduce noise and vibration. Restful quiet is as much a part of the Mercury's comfort as its soft, deep seats. • The Mercury has precision-built hydraulic brakes, and a brilliant, economical 95-horsepower V-type 8-cylinder engine. All Mercury appointments are as modern as the new steering wheel and instrument panel shown at right.

Ford exhibits at Two Great Fairs this year — New York and San Francisco

FEATURES OF THE MERCURY 8
116-inch wheelbase; 16 feet, 4 inches over-all length • Unusual width and room for passengers • 95-hp. V-type 8-cylinder engine • Hydraulic brakes • Modern flowing lines • Luxurious appointments and upholstery • Deep, soft seat construction • Thorough scientific soundproofing • Balanced weight distribution and center-poise design • Unusually large luggage compartments.
FORD-BUILT MEANS TOP VALUE

1938 MERCURY, convertible coupe

1939 BANTAM, roadster, 2-passenger

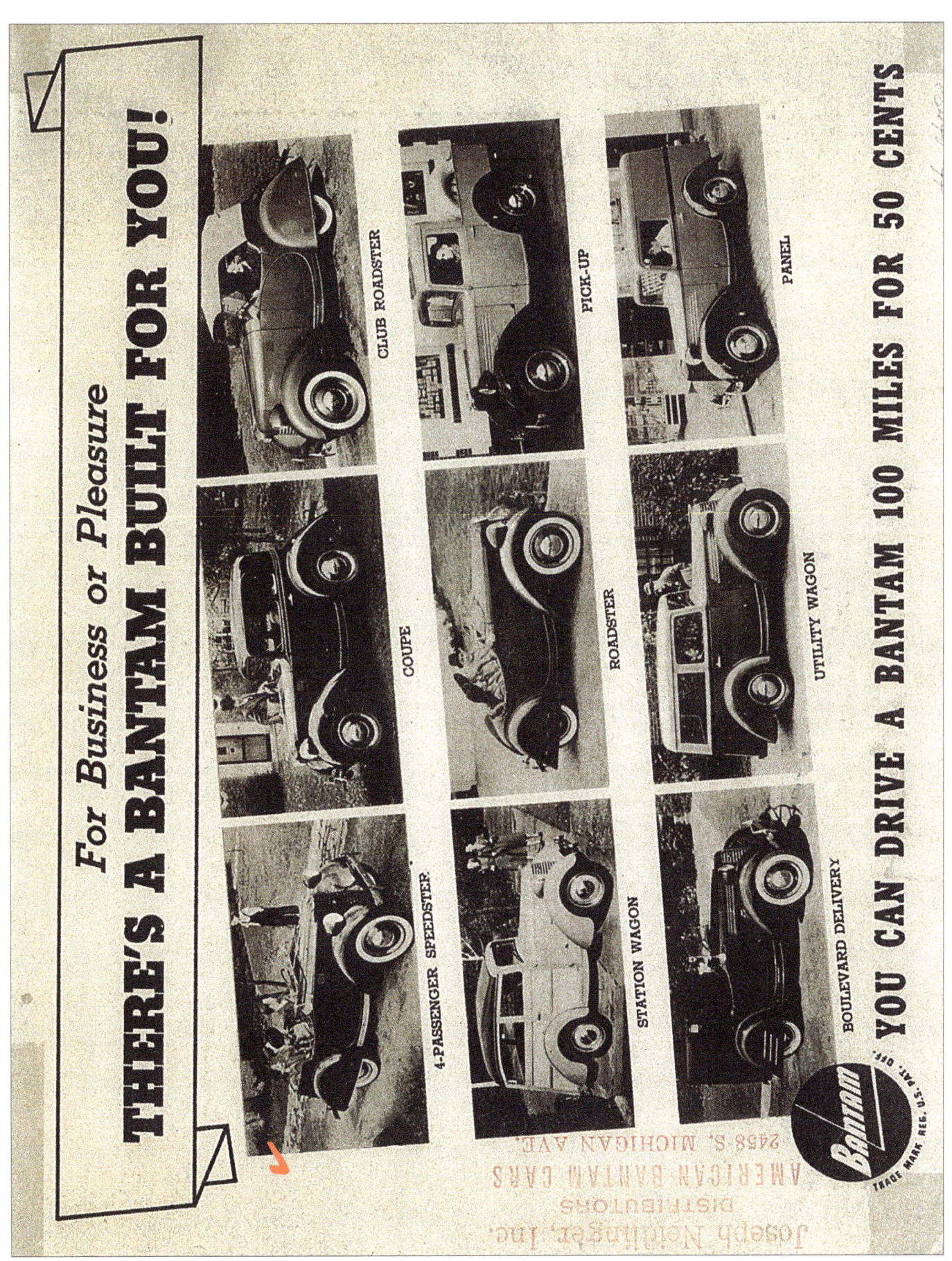

1939 BANTAM, speedster, 4-passenger (3 cars)

| AMERICA'S ONLY ECONOMY CAR | # The Bantam NEWS | AMERICA'S LOWEST PRICE CAR |

VOL. 1, No. 1.   BUTLER, PENNSYLVANIA.   JULY, 1938

BANTAM ANNOUNCES

SIXTY-SIX MAJOR REFINEMENTS AND IMPROVEMENTS SERVE TO BRING EXTRA QUALITY TO CARS

If you are not one of the 400 dealers now making money with Bantam—mail the coupon on page eight.

4-PASSENGER CAR, BOULEVARD DELIVERY, STATION WAGON ARE ADDED TO PRESENT BANTAM LINE

PRESENTING THE FOURSOME

Brilliant pacemaker of the Bantam line is the new four-passenger speedster. Designed as a thrifty car for the average family, its smartness makes a tremendous appeal to the style-conscious younger set.

By F. H. FENN, Vice-President

During the 6 months Bantam has been in production, engineers have been experimenting and working to further improve Bantam cars and trucks. As a result of these experiments, and from the suggestions of dealers and customers, 66 distinct improvements have been incorporated in the second series Bantam "60."

Bantam has developed an oil sealed engine that banishes oil leakage and guarantees oil economy. Improved carburetion not only gives greater economy but also provides faster get-away and more power on hills.

F. H. FENN

The newly developed super-silent ball bearing fan is greased for life, assuring trouble-free engine cooling and noiseless operation. Bodies are Spray-Texed completely. Form fitting, sound proofed floor mats and a new noiseless muffler add to the quiet smoothness of Bantam operation.

Interior appointments and upholstering redesigned by Count Alexis deSahknoffsky, foremost exponent of modern streamlining, give new beauty and comfort to the cars. The hand brake lever is now placed more conveniently providing greater foot room and easier handling.

All passenger cars now offer a high speed rear end and Quickaway traffic transmission giving greater economy and higher cruising speeds.

Trucks are now provided with a specially designed truck gear. A new smooth acting clutch gives greater ease of operation.

Australia To Get New Bantam Plant

Bantam will enter the Australian market this summer with an engine and chassis assembly and body building plant in Sydney, as a result of a contract signed with W. H. Cameron, managing director of Car Productions, Pty., Ltd., and associated Australian companies.

Because resources in iron and coal make Australia an ideal manufacturing country, bodies will be built complete in Australia, including all stamping and welding operations. Tires will also be of Australian manufacture.

Engine and chassis parts, however, will be built and machined in the Bantam plant and shipped unassembled to the Sydney factory.

The initial outlay in the Australian Bantam plant will be $250,000 with an expected eventual investment of $1,000,000.

Plant Enlargement Is Now Completed At Butler Factory

A comprehensive program of plant improvement and enlargement has just been completed at the Bantam factory.

In order to meet the rising demand for Bantam cars and trucks, it was necessary to increase the size of the Body Building Division in order to bring the capacity of this department nearer that of the chassis and engine line, the latter being capable of producing 200 units a day.

Equipment for an entirely new method of painting cars is being installed in the factory. Bantam is the first company to use this new principle for which many advantages are claimed.

No matter what car you handle today you can step up your profits amazingly with Bantam. See the coupon on the back page.

Smart Distributors Make Record Sales

Ten 8-Bantam carloads in seven weeks is the good news flashing from I. Benoit, Ltd., Bantam distributor in the Province of Quebec. McNaughton Motor Sales of Winnipeg, a new distributor, has taken 3 carloads in two weeks.

In the United States, Bantam Distributors of New York have rung up a record of 11 carloads in 9 weeks. P. W. White Motors of St. Louis, have averaged a carload a week during their three weeks as Bantam distributors. W. M. Duvall in Tulsa, has taken 3 carloads in two and a half weeks.

In Florida, more than 100 Bantams have been sold with no sign of the usual summer slump. In all, more than 400 distributors and dealers are finding Bantam an excellent sales booster.

By ROY S. EVANS, President

Three new models, packed with sales appeal and greatly broadening the Bantam market, are included in the fast-selling offerings in the second series Bantam "60."

The Foursome, a swank new four-passenger job, puts its rakish contours in the lead position of the three new models, giving Bantam a high-stepping, low-priced entry into the great market of the 4-to-the-family motor car buyers. Smartly designed and restfully cushioned, the Foursome which sells in the $400 price range, makes a commanding bow to the average size, average income family.

ROY S. EVANS

Streamlined from the radiator ornament on her eager prow to the final flare of the rear fenders, the Foursome puts a new meaning to style. Ingenious interior arrangements give surprising comfort to four full-sized passengers.

We are frank to admit that the dashing lines of the Foursome are copied from the smart European small open 4-seaters which, although costing nearly twice as much as Bantam, are nevertheless the continent's largest sellers.

The leisurely luxury of Newport is bred in every line of the gay new Bantam Station Wagon. The body gleams with the polished grain of maple, carefully wrought by the craft of experienced cabinet makers whose skill shows in every contour of the spacious body.

(Continued on Page 2)

THE STATION WAGON

Smart enough for Southampton, sturdy enough for the farm, the gay Bantam Station Wagon serves as a four-passenger car and, by the easy removal of the rear seat, converts into a practical light-hauling u[nit].

BOULEVARD DELIVERY

A jewel box on wheels, this distinctive vehicle combines the nostalgic splendor of the Hansom cab with the suave dignity of milady's limousine. Economy, smartness and traffic ag[ility mak]e the Boulevard Delivery ideal for smart shops.

1939 BANTAM, station wagon

1939 BANTAM, pickup truck

1939 BANTAM, Speedster and station wagon

BANTAM, panel truck

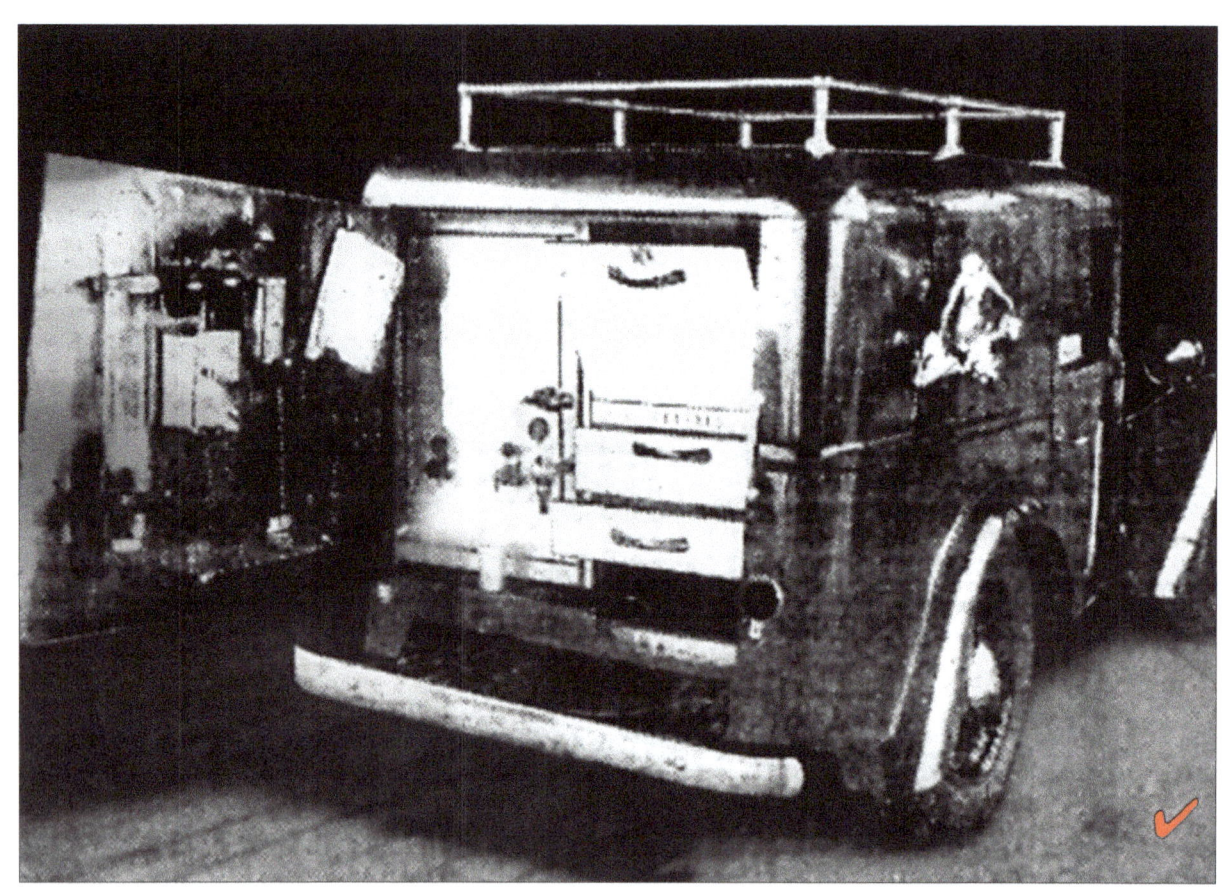

1939 BANTAM, panel truck conversion into a "BROCK "Dinky Diner".

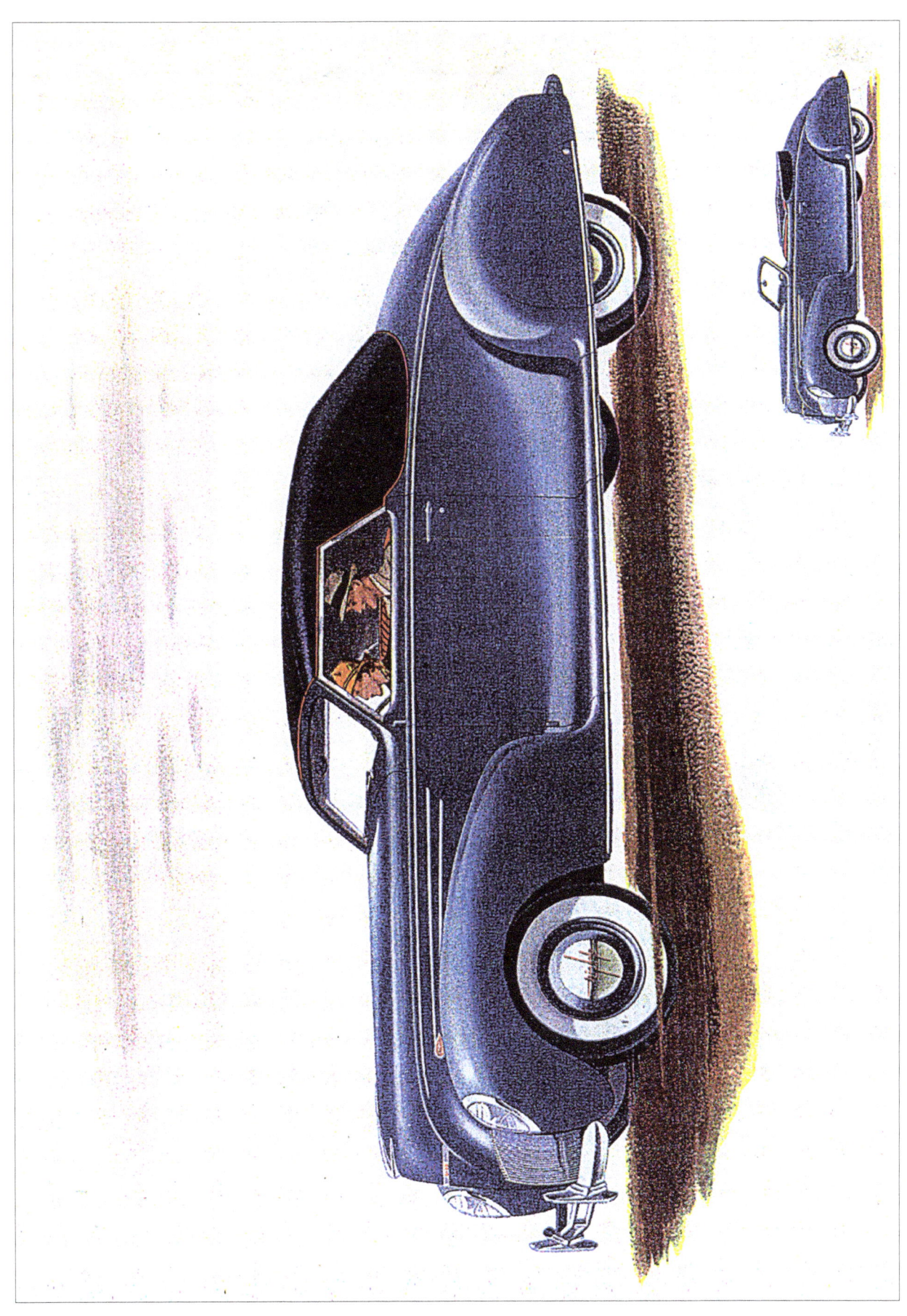

1939 LINCOLN ZEPHYR, convertible coupe

1939 LINCOLN CONTINENTAL, convertible coupe

Friends of the Wind

THERE'S true kinship with the wind in every flowing line of the new 1941 Lincoln-Continental. Completely streamlined from the inside out, it cleaves the rushing currents of air cleanly and quietly in its smooth, effortless gliding flight. You seem to ride on the wings of the wind!

SKILLED craftsmen in the great Lincoln plant have created for the staunch, power-charged, 12-cylinder heart of the Lincoln-Continental a long, luxurious, low-slung body that surpasses all previous conceptions of automotive beauty. Here is a car almost daringly young—so decidedly *different* in design and construction you know at a glance it's styled for you who want unstinted luxury tempered with good taste . . .

IN PERFECT keeping with such sheer splendor—such unusual performance—is the comfort of billowy seats cradled amidships on liquid-like, slow-motion springs. And the Lincoln-Continental is triple-cushioned in rubber to block out noise and vibration . . . gives you a ride as smooth and quiet as a glider's flight.

BEFORE you buy any car make a date with your dealer and go for a ride in the new Lincoln-Continental. See how it hugs the curves, holds snugly to the road and cuts the air like a bullet. Delight in the brilliant performance and lithe streamlining that make it truly a "friend of the wind." You'll discover, at last, the thrill of driving a car that's altogether *new* and *unusual*.

Suave, sleek masterpiece in steel and luxury, the Lincoln-Continental Coupe shown above combines a host of unusual automotive comforts, conveniences and betterments: Exclusive Lincoln V-12 engine . . . push-button door openers . . . unit body-and-frame construction. (White sidewall tires extra.) ¶ Interiors are custom-tailored. You choose from a wide range of fabrics and leathers. ¶ Smart Convertible Cabriolet also available. Every feature of the dynamic *nete-and-differ*-Lincoln-Continental will convince you that here, indeed, is a limited edition of a fine motor car.

LINCOLN MOTOR CAR DIVISION, FORD MOTOR COMPANY, BUILDERS ALSO OF THE LINCOLN-ZEPHYR V-12, SEDAN, COUPE, CLUB COUPE, CONVERTIBLE COUPE, THE LINCOLN-CUSTOM, SEDAN AND LIMOUSINE

1941 LINCOLN CONTINENTAL, 2-door sedan

The Harley-Davidson "74" Twin

Recognized everywhere as the world's standard motorcycle, with 26 years of progress behind it, the "74" Twin today stands head and shoulders above all comers. For 1930 this famous Twin has been completely re-designed from stem to stern . . . new motor, new frame, new forks, new wheels, new tanks, new generator, everything new! For solo or sidecar riding the new "74" Twin asks no favors of anything on the road.

The new "74" Twin motor, designed along the lines of the "45" that proved such an outstanding success last season, is exceptionally accessible, clean and dependable. Its genuine Ricardo heads are scientifically designed to provide the correct turbulence of compressed gases and assure quick, complete combustion. They are easily detachable for carbon removal and valve grinding.

For 1930 the "74" frame has been strengthened at all vital points. It is now at least 100% stronger. The saddle position is two inches lower, and the large capacity tanks are shorter and wider. Double-strength drop forged sides feature the 1930 front forks. They are built to stand the hardest service.

Quick detachable, interchangeable wheels are standard on the "74" Twin for 1930. This exclusive Harley-Davidson feature is especially valuable in combination with the sidecar. Drop-center rims and big, 4" full balloon tires complete the equipment.

Many new advancements for 1930 — added to the time-tried and proved features of former models — have made the "74," more than ever, the greatest motorcycle value ever offered.

◆

Model 30V, 74 cubic inch Twin, fitted with nickel iron pistons, $340 at factory. Model 30VL, fitted with Dow metal pistons and high compression cylinder heads, $340 at factory. Model 30VS, for sidecar use, fitted with nickel iron pistons, standard compression heads and sidecar gearing, $340 at factory.

1943 — 1930 HARLEY-DAVIDSON, motorcycle, model #30VL

You name it... the 'JEEP' does it

The "Jeep" power take-off operates a winch or serves any number of other useful purposes. With spline shaft or pulley drive, it furnishes mobile power for many kinds of industrial and agricultural units.

The "Jeep" makes a handy, economical pick-up unhampered by close quarters or bad roads. You use conventional 2-wheel drive for highway speed and economy; sure-footed 4-wheel drive for heavy going.

There seems to be no limit to what you can do with a "Jeep" —the versatile, all-purpose vehicle that serves all industry.

It carries up to 800 pounds or pulls up to 2½ tons across town or across the plant yard. It gets in and out of places where less maneuverable vehicles cannot go. It threads its way right into your plant... takes material directly to the production line... delivers finished products for shipment or storage. It doubles as tow truck, service car, pick-up.

As a runabout, the Universal "Jeep" takes repair men and maintenance crews wherever their work requires, traveling on or off the road with equal ease and delivering men, tools, and power directly to the job.

The "Jeep" serves also as a mobile power unit—with power take-offs that deliver up to 30 hp for the operation of industrial equipment or agricultural units.

Ask your Willys-Overland dealer to demonstrate the "Jeep" right on the job, and see for yourself how "Jeep" versatility can be used in *your* business.

WILLYS-OVERLAND MOTORS, INC., TOLEDO 1, O.
Maker of America's Most Useful Vehicles

GET A 'Jeep'

1946 JEEP, CJ2A, civilian Jeep

1946 WILLYS, 'Jeep' station wagon

"DOUBLING IN BRASS"

...Just Another Way of Saying That the "Jeep" Helps Out In More Ways Than One!

When drifts pile high, the Universal "Jeep" doubles in brass as a snow plow. The hydraulic-lift snow blade is installed in just a few minutes and with 4-wheel-drive for traction on icy roads, the highly maneuverable "Jeep" handles snow-removal work for service stations, manufacturing concerns and street departments.

But best of all—when one job is done, the Universal "Jeep" is ready for another! It answers emergency calls...powers welders, compressors and sprayers ...works indoors or out as an industrial tractor... operates on or off the road in any weather. See this versatile vehicle at Willys-Overland dealers.

THE UNIVERSAL 'Jeep'

WILLYS-OVERLAND MOTORS, INC., TOLEDO, OHIO
MAKERS OF AMERICA'S MOST USEFUL VEHICLES

1948 JEEP, CJ2A, civilian Jeep

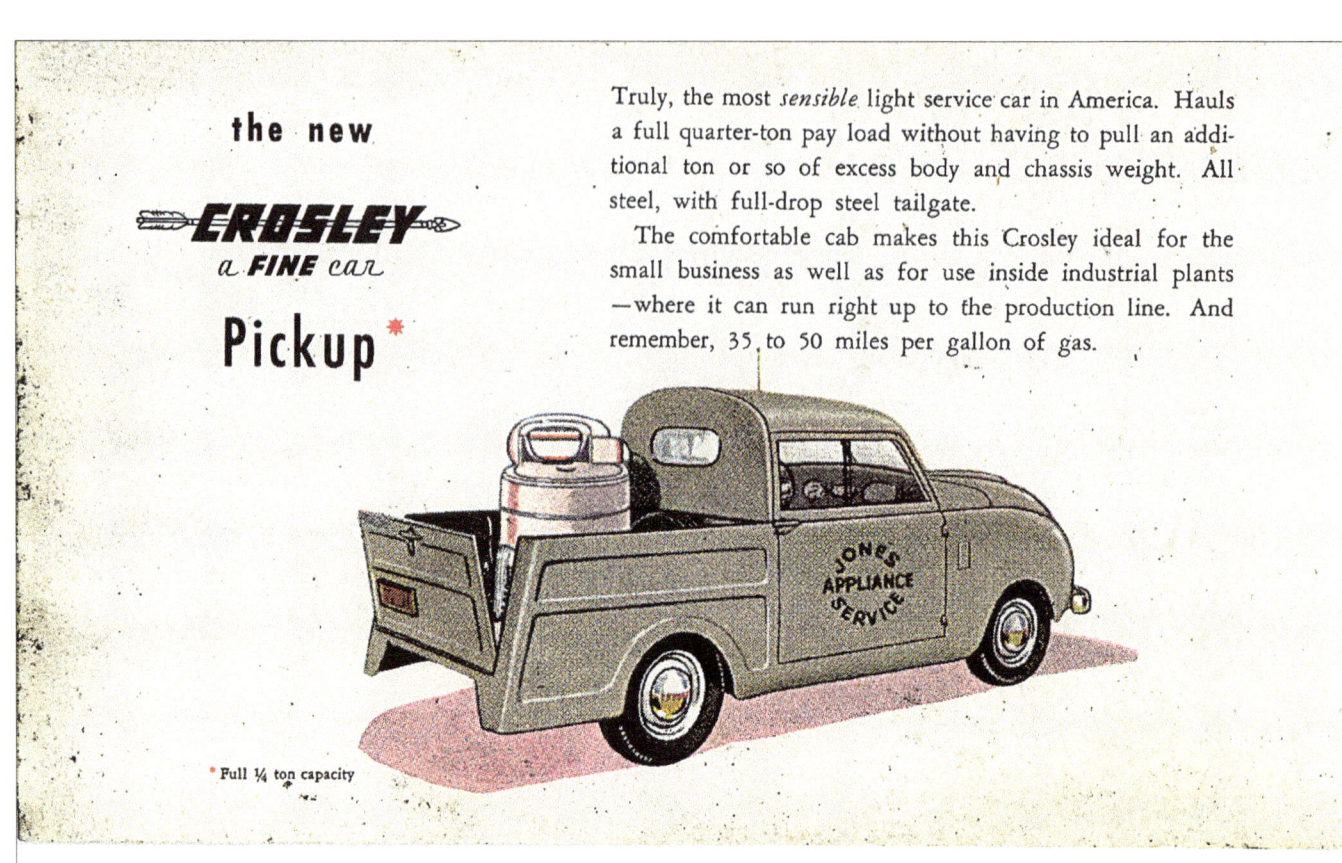

the new
Crosley
a FINE car
Pickup*

Truly, the most *sensible* light service car in America. Hauls a full quarter-ton pay load without having to pull an additional ton or so of excess body and chassis weight. All steel, with full-drop steel tailgate.

The comfortable cab makes this Crosley ideal for the small business as well as for use inside industrial plants —where it can run right up to the production line. And remember, 35 to 50 miles per gallon of gas.

* Full ¼ ton capacity

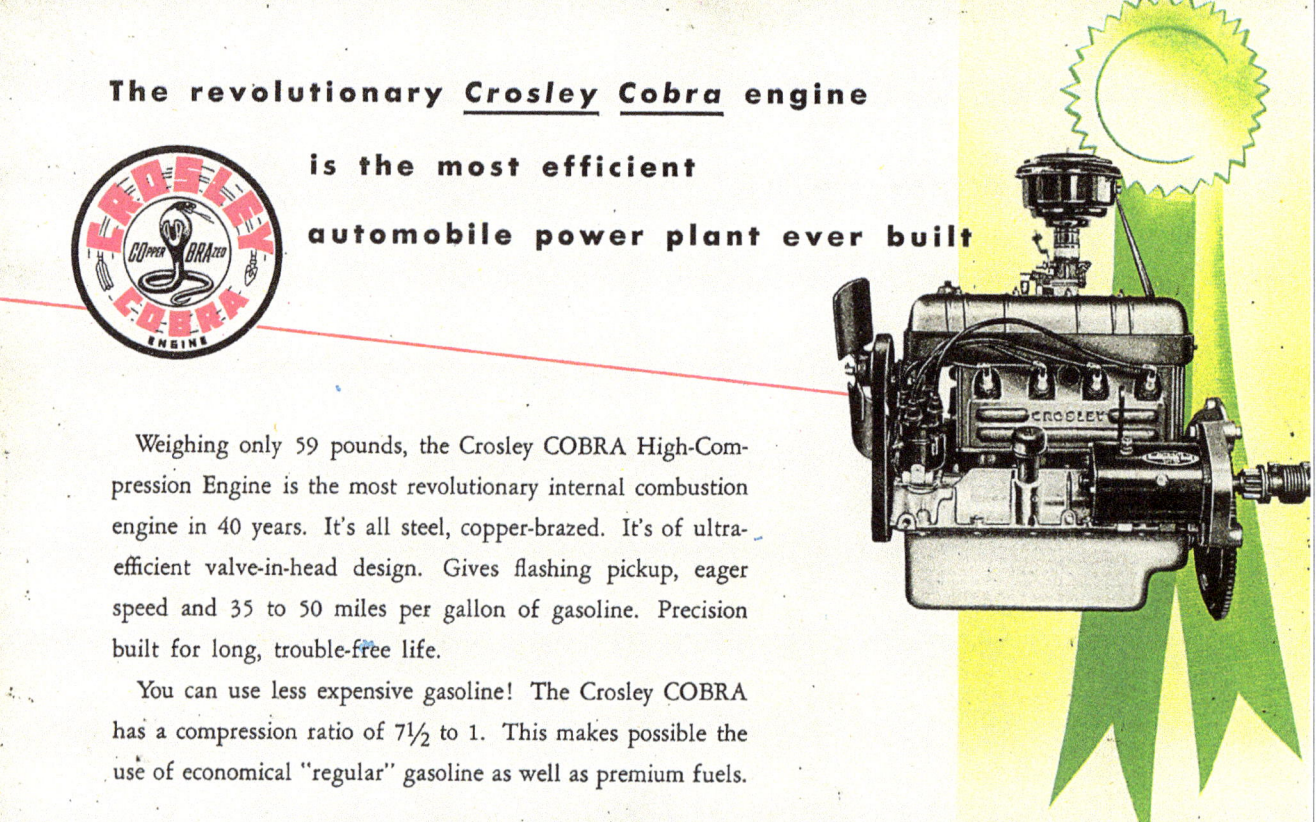

The revolutionary *Crosley Cobra* engine is the most efficient automobile power plant ever built

Weighing only 59 pounds, the Crosley COBRA High-Compression Engine is the most revolutionary internal combustion engine in 40 years. It's all steel, copper-brazed. It's of ultra-efficient valve-in-head design. Gives flashing pickup, eager speed and 35 to 50 miles per gallon of gasoline. Precision built for long, trouble-free life.

You can use less expensive gasoline! The Crosley COBRA has a compression ratio of 7½ to 1. This makes possible the use of economical "regular" gasoline as well as premium fuels.

1948 CROSLEY, pickup truck

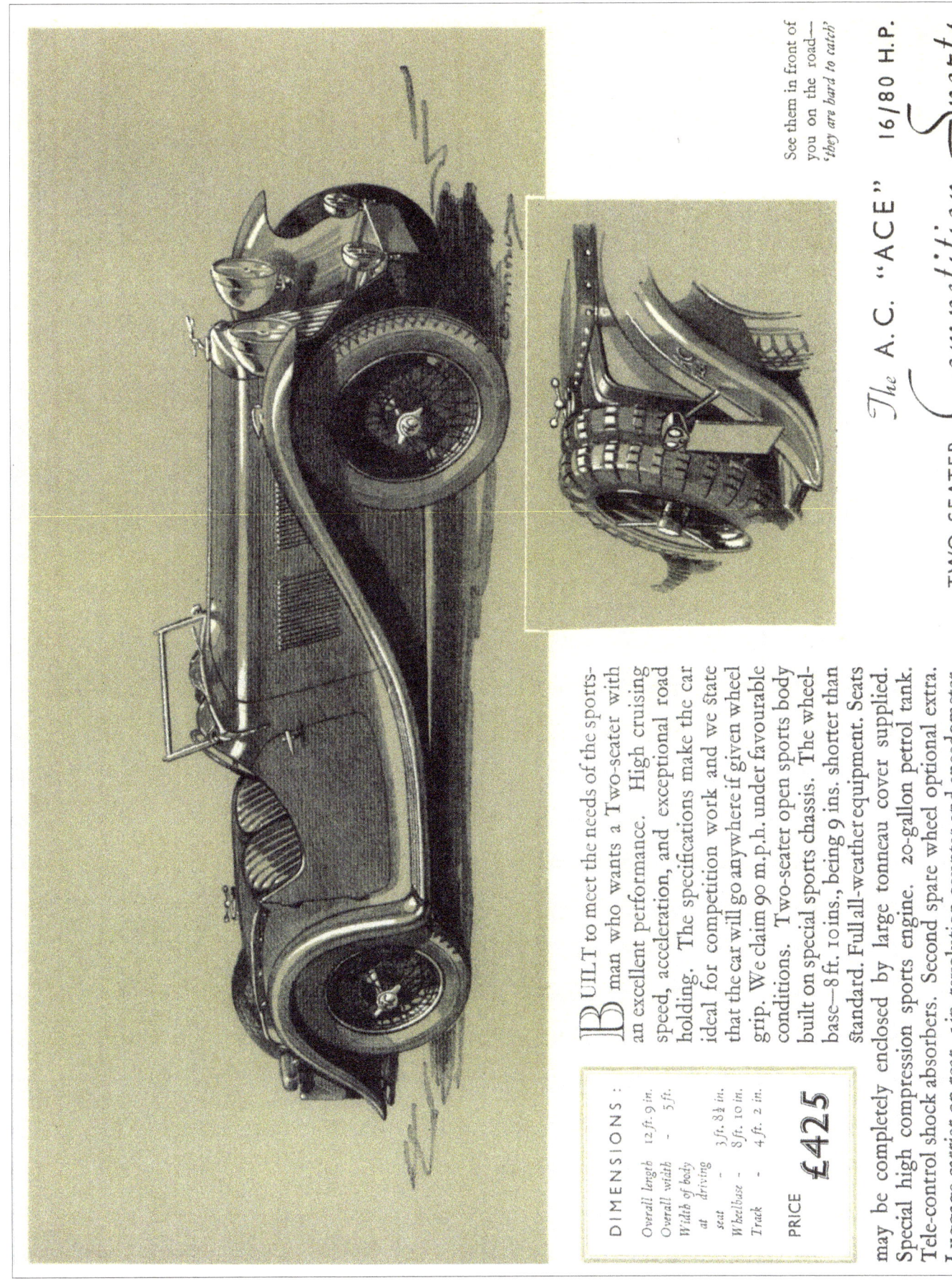

1948 — 1937 AC, Ace, 16/80, sports car, purchased used

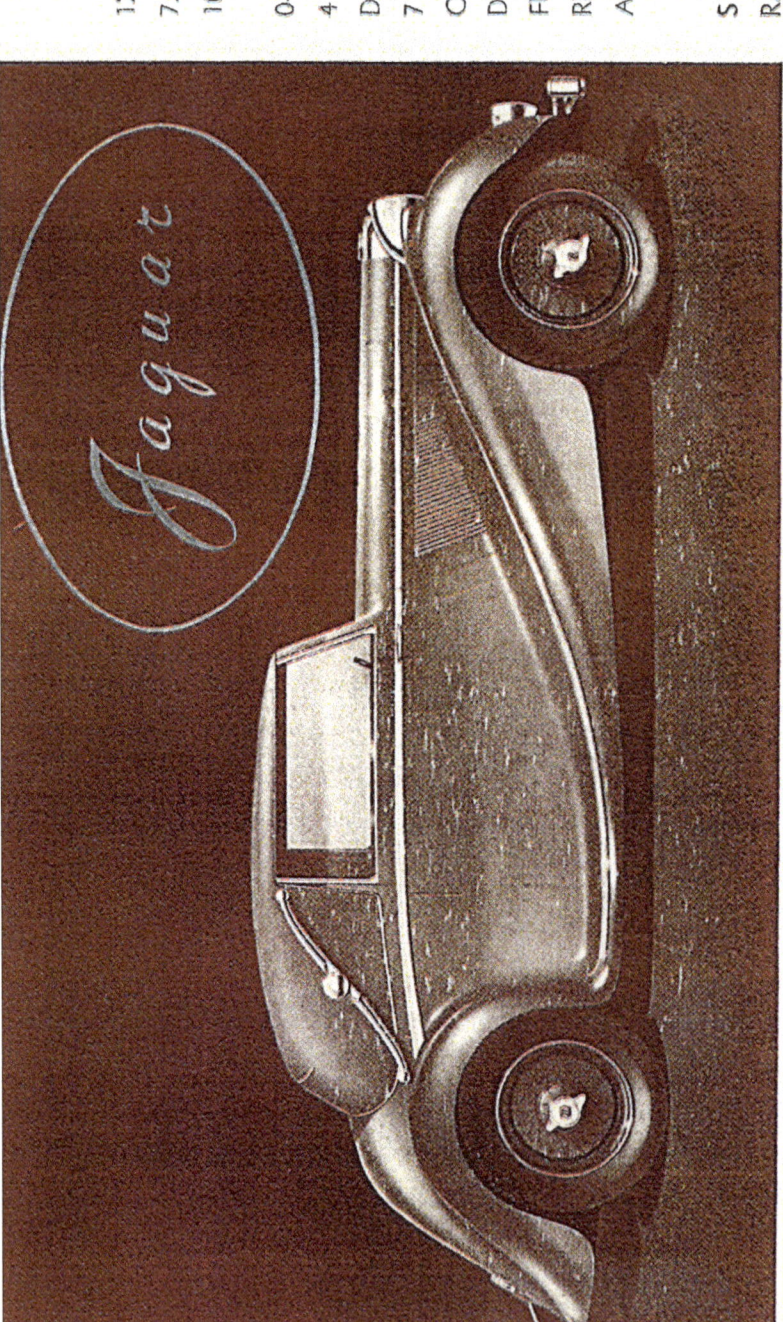

3½ LITRE JAGUAR

- 125 BRAKE HORSEPOWER
- 7.2 COMPRESSION RATIO
- 100 M.P.H. PERFORMANCE (Electrically Timed)
- 0-50 M.P.H. IN 9.5 SECONDS
- 4 SPEED TRANSMISSION
- DUAL CARBURATION
- 7 BEARING CRANKSHAFT
- OVERHEAD VALVES
- DUAL ELECTRIC FUEL PUMPS
- FULL FLOW OIL FILTER
- RESERVE GAS TANK
- AIRFOAM SEATS

STANDARD EQUIPMENT

- RACING TYPE WHEELS
- FOG LIGHTS
- WHEEL DISCS
- HEATER
- JAGUAR RADIATOR MASCOT
- ELABORATE TOOL KIT
- KIT OF SPARE PARTS
- TOP BOOT
- TELESCOPIC STEERING COLUMN
- TWIN ELECTRIC WINDSHIELD WIPER
- TWIN TUNED HORNS
- SPECIAL JACKING SYSTEM

INTERNATIONAL MOTORS, INC.

"The Foreign Car Specialists"

SHOP
8741 ALDEN DRIVE, LOS ANGELES 36
(One block South of Beverly Boulevard)
(East of Robertson Boulevard)
BRadshaw 2-1303
CRestview 1-8694

SHOWROOM
8536 SUNSET BOULEVARD
HOLLYWOOD 46
"On the Sunset Strip"
CRestview 5-4005
Open Evenings and Sundays

1948 JAGUAR, Mark IV, 2-door convertible, spare tire on trunk

1948 (Wright's customized 1940 LINCOLN CONTINENTAL, convertible)

1949 JAGUAR, Mark V, 4-door sedan

CROSLEY LEADS AGAIN
...with America's own sport car!

THE CROSLEY Hotshot

ROAD AND TRACK RACING CAR!

For those who want to get into track racing, road racing or hill climbing competitions, the high-powered CIBA engine may be souped up as high as 12 or 14-to-1 compression ratio. In addition, windshield, bumpers, top and headlights are removable. Quickly detachable side doors, not shown, as well as all-weather, tailored top and side curtains are standard equipment.

It's here—a new thrill in motoring, a new pace-setter for the whole Crosley line. It's the new Crosley Hotshot, swank as the smartest European custom jobs—but it delivers for $1,500 to $3,500 less. Yes, the Hotshot is actually priced even lower than other Crosley passenger models!

And what a car! A dashing two-seater, long, sleek, with dropped frame, road clearance of 7-inches and deep, comfortable, aircraft type seats. The Hotshot has combined leaf and coil spring rear suspension and strut-type hydraulic shock absorbers all around to give smooth, shock-free road hugging ability necessary in racing type vehicles. It's the big opportunity in today's market—a unique style leader priced well under a thousand dollars!

COMPLETE LINE — 6 MODELS

The Crosley dealer has a model to meet every taste, every need. His line now includes everything—ultra-smart sport car, family cars and trucks too!

CROSLEY SEDAN DELUXE
A designer's dream, modern speedline styling, sweep fenders. Rich interior, choice fabric upholstery. Seats 4 with ample luggage room.

CROSLEY STATION WAGON
Larger, longer body lines, new luxury interior appointments. Seats 4, or 2 with ¼ ton load. All steel.

CROSLEY CONVERTIBLE
Seats 4. Big luggage compartment. The easy-to-handle top can be raised or lowered in a jiffy.

CROSLEY PANEL DELIVERY
Smartest delivery truck on the streets. Operates for about ½ as much as other trucks. ¼ ton capacity.

CROSLEY PICK-UP TRUCK
Heavy-duty type stamina. Slips through traffic easily, turns in a 15 foot radius. Carries ¼ ton load with 2 in roomy cab.

CROSLEY MOTORS, INC.
DEPT. 95, 2530 SPRING GROVE AVE.
CINCINNATI 14, OHIO

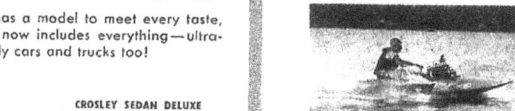

World's record made by CROSLEY powered speedboat!
A Crosley powered hydroplane, piloted by Jack Van Deman, of Philadelphia, recently established a new world's record of 52.250 miles per hour. The 44 cu. in. speedster cracked all records in establishing this 48 cu. in. record.

CROSLEY — first in the world with the world's safest brakes!

HYDRADISC (AIRPLANE TYPE HYDRAULIC) BRAKES

Hydradisc Brakes are new, revolutionary hydraulic brakes of the type used on the biggest and fastest commercial and military planes. These brakes were invented by Hawley, licensed to Goodyear, engineered and developed by them in conjunction with the military air force to meet the necessity for positive braking on the heavy and fast modern aircraft. They give positive braking action even under the worst conditions—water, mud, slush, ice or oil. One simple external screw adjustment—long-lived braking material.

CIBA (CAST-IRON BLOCK) ENGINE

Heart of the Hotshot is the amazing CIBA (cast-iron block) engine that now powers all Crosley cars. Built with an overhead camshaft, the CIBA is the only light, high-speed, high-compression, racing type engine mass-produced in the U. S. It's 4-cylinder, quiet running, long-lived.

A leader in economy, the CIBA goes up to 50 miles on a gallon of regular gasoline.

And these are only two among hundreds of other Crosley improvements—ranging from spiral bevel gears and valve rotators to undercoating.

a FINE car

You see them everywhere!

DISTRIBUTORS AND ADDITIONAL DEALERS are now being appointed. If you are interested in selling a proven car to the vast market which exists at around $1,000, where there is no competition, write, wire or telephone at once to W. A. MacDonald, Fred R. Cooper, or Stanley E. Kess, Sales Vice President.

1949 CROSLEY, Hotshot roadster (2 cars)

BORG-WARNER HAS BEEN WORKING HAND IN HAND WITH CROSLEY FROM THE START!

"For extra quality and ruggedness, we have Borg-Warner make certain essential operating parts to our own specifications."

PRESIDENT, CROSLEY MOTORS, INC.

Almost every American benefits every day from the 185 products of

BORG-WARNER

created for the automotive, aviation, marine, farm implement, and home appliance industries.

At present, more than 60,000 Crosleys are on the road. And Borg-Warner is proud of its association with this car which can claim from 35 to 50 miles per gallon of gasoline—and actually weighs only one-third as much as other light cars.

But this is only one phase of B-W's association with the automotive industry. Today, 19 of the 20 makes of cars contain one or more basic working parts from Borg-Warner. Such parts as transmissions, automatic overdrives, clutches, universal joints, propeller shafts, radiators and timing chains.

Car manufacturers like Borg-Warner's big-scale facilities and highly developed engineering skills. They appreciate, too, B-W's constant objective: "design it better—make it better."

The result is a working partnership which promises for you an even finer "car of tomorrow."

These units form BORG-WARNER, Executive Offices, 310 South Michigan Ave., Chicago: BORG & BECK • BORG-WARNER INTERNATIONAL • BORG WARNER SERVICE PARTS • CALUMET STEEL • DETROIT GEAR • DETROIT VAPOR STOVE • FRANKLIN STEEL • INGERSOLL STEEL • INGERSOLL UTILITY UNIT • LONG MANUFACTURING • LONG MANUFACTURING CO., LTD. • MARBON • MARVEL-SCHEBLER CARBURETER • MECHANICS UNIVERSAL JOINT • MORSE CHAIN • MORSE CHAIN CO., LTD. • NORGE • NORGE-HEAT • NORGE MACHINE PRODUCTS • PESCO PRODUCTS • ROCKFORD CLUTCH • SPRING DIVISION • SUPERIOR SHEET STEEL • WARNER AUTOMOTIVE PARTS • WARNER GEAR • WARNER GEAR CO., LTD.

1949 CROSLEY, station wagon

The CROSLEY Hotshot

original art by **COUNT ALEXIS DE SAKHNOFFSKY**

America's own sport car!

...swank as the smartest European custom jobs—but American, all American. High in style, amazingly low in price—even less than other Crosley passenger models. Actually delivers for $1,500 to $3,500 less than the price of similar types developed by European manufacturers.

A dashing two-seater, sleek as an arrow, the Crosley Hotshot will draw a crowd on Main Street or at the club.

The Hotshot is a sophisticated car, light, fast, economical.

It's designed to give the young in spirit, from 17 to 70, a new experience in motoring. With its dropped frame, low center of gravity, road clearance of 7 inches, and deep, comfortable aircraft type seats, it offers the thrill of moving swiftly and safely close to the ground.

When you see the beautiful new Hotshot, you'll want to drive it. And when you drive it, you'll want to own it!

1950 CROSLEY, Hotshot roadster (3 cars)

1950 CROSLEY, Super station wagon (2 cars)

Major Improvements in CROSLEY for 1951

These make the Crosley the *most improved car* for 1951 — the greatest assembly of improvements ever put into a new Crosley model.

New strut type hydraulic shock absorbers
New, big 9 inch Bendix hydraulic brakes
New heavy duty front axle
New larger, easily adjustable clutch
Cast iron block
New mechanical link clutch release mechanism
New exhaust valve rotators for longer engine life
New full flow oil filter
New seats with improved cushions and pads
New full-fashioned floor mats
New interior upholstery and trim
Turn indicators
New improved hand brake control
Radically new front design combined with late restyling of body
Roll-down windows
New-tailored upholstery on door panels
Fold-up rear seats
Folding top (Super Sports)

1951 SUPER STATION WAGON

All steel. Rear seat folds forward or is removable for extra luggage space. Roll-down windows. Seats 4, or 2 with ¼ ton load. New basket-weave design on wagon panels. Deluxe appointments.

1951 CROSLEY, station wagon

1951 CROSLEY, Farm-O-Road, dual rear wheels

Every inch a Riley-

In these days when cars tend to be more and more alike, Riley stands out as typically British. Distinctive styling, responsive performance and excellent road-holding are some of the attributes which ensure " MAGNIFICENT MOTORING."

Yet Riley character goes deeper still, it has been built up through progressive generations of discriminating enthusiasts, it has achieved that indefinable quality built into the car that is as 'old as the industry, as modern as the hour'.

100 h.p. 2½ litre Saloon £958.   Purchase Tax £266. 17. 2.   1½ litre Saloon £714.   Purchase Tax £199.1. 8.

FOR MAGNIFICENT MOTORING

See the Riley models at the Motor Show, Earls Court.

1951 RILEY, RMB, 4-door sedan

1952 MG-TD, 2-passenger sports car

1952 AUSTIN, Somerset, A40, 4-door sedan

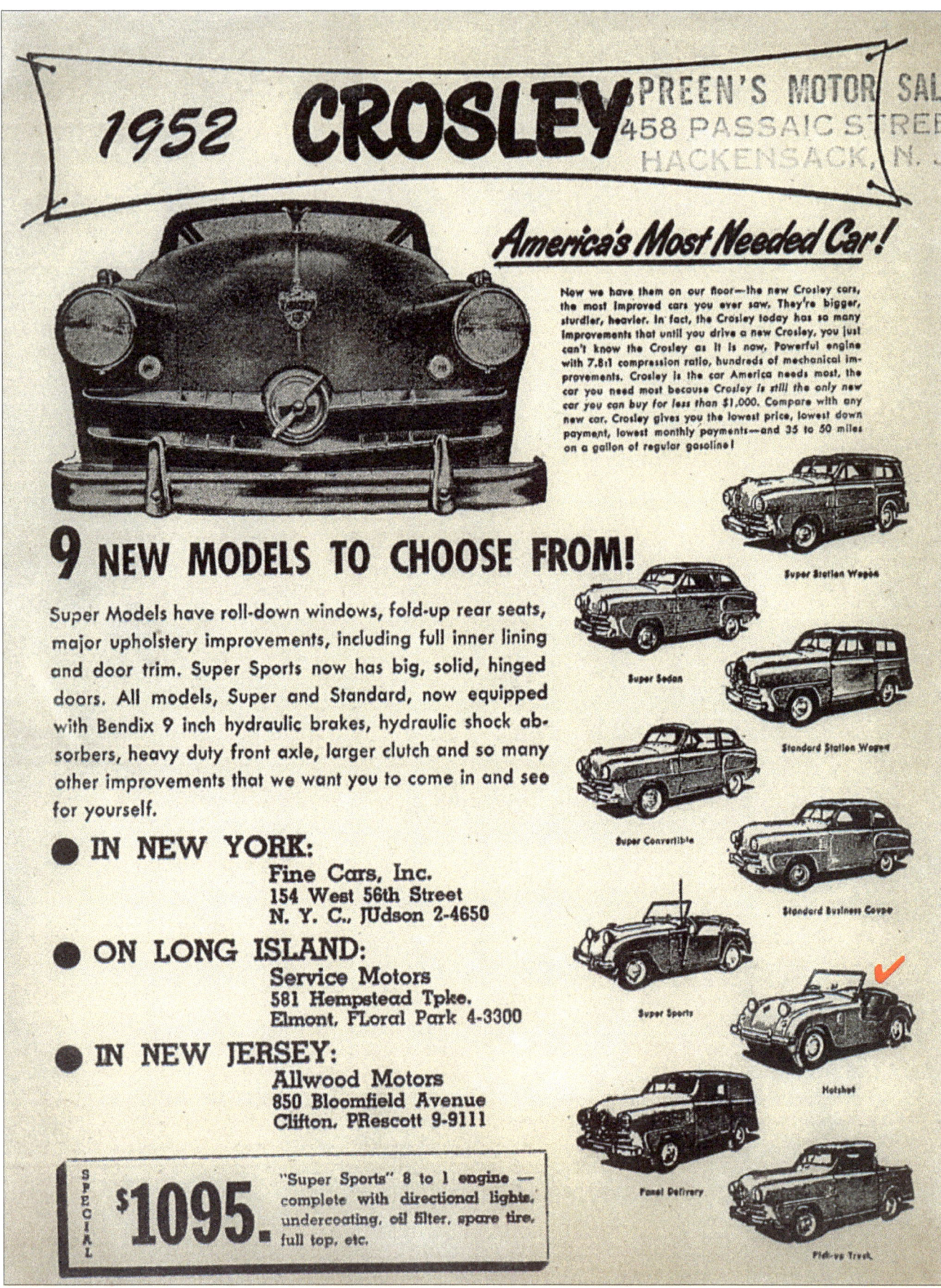

1952 CROSLEY, Supersport (6 cars)

1952 HILLMAN MINX, convertible, 3 way top (3 cars)

1952 HILLMAN MINX, 4-door sedan (3 cars)

1952 — 1929 CORD, L-29, 2-door Cabriolet, purchased used

1953 FORD, Victoria, 2-door hardtop

1953 FORD, Country Squire, station wagon

1953 FORD, Ranch Wagon, 2-door, station wagon

1953 PONTIAC, Catalina, 2-door, hardtop

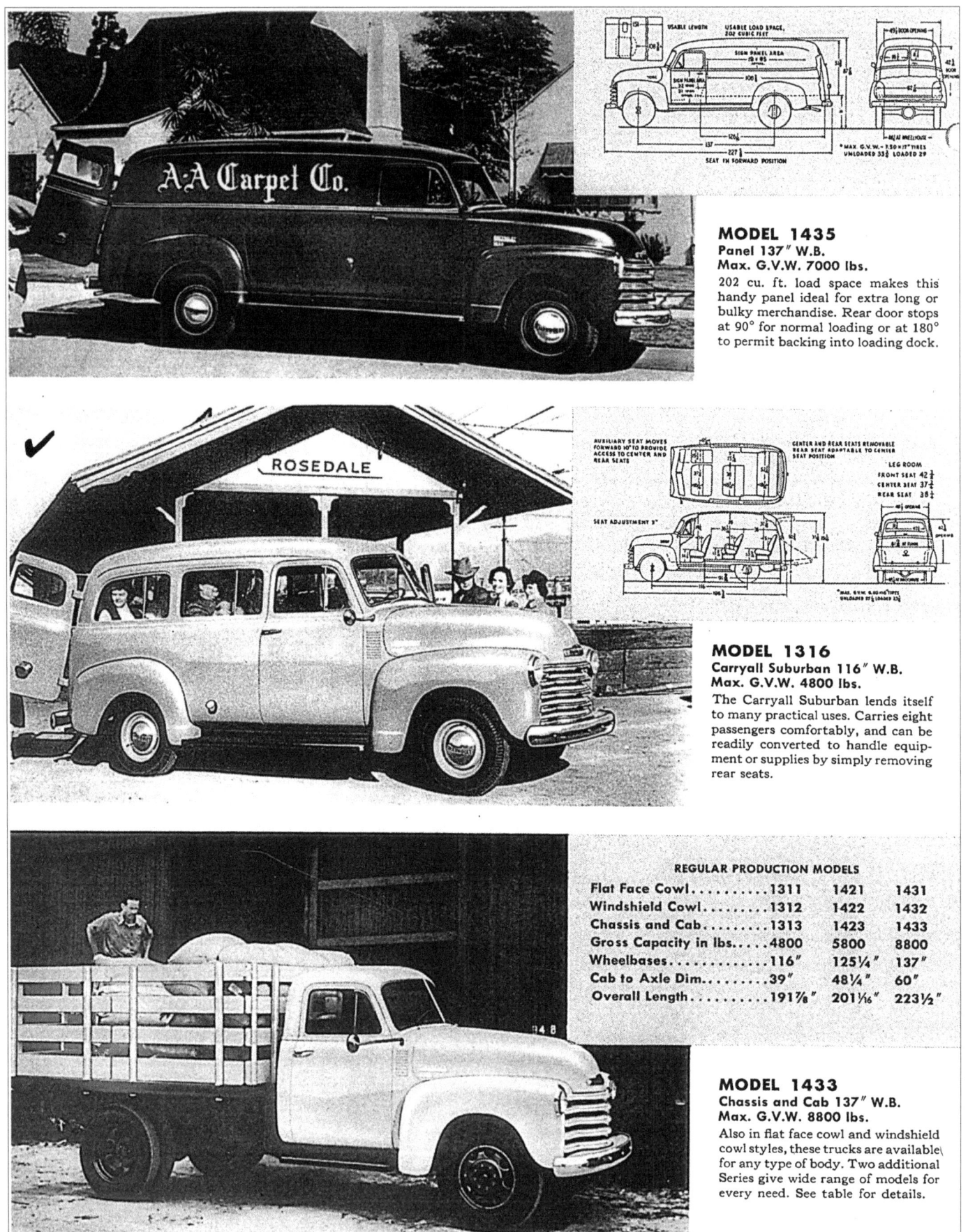

MODEL 1435
Panel 137" W.B.
Max. G.V.W. 7000 lbs.
202 cu. ft. load space makes this handy panel ideal for extra long or bulky merchandise. Rear door stops at 90° for normal loading or at 180° to permit backing into loading dock.

MODEL 1316
Carryall Suburban 116" W.B.
Max. G.V.W. 4800 lbs.
The Carryall Suburban lends itself to many practical uses. Carries eight passengers comfortably, and can be readily converted to handle equipment or supplies by simply removing rear seats.

REGULAR PRODUCTION MODELS			
Flat Face Cowl	1311	1421	1431
Windshield Cowl	1312	1422	1432
Chassis and Cab	1313	1423	1433
Gross Capacity in lbs.	4800	5800	8800
Wheelbases	116"	125¼"	137"
Cab to Axle Dim.	39"	48¼"	60"
Overall Length	191⅞"	201 1/16"	223½"

MODEL 1433
Chassis and Cab 137" W.B.
Max. G.V.W. 8800 lbs.
Also in flat face cowl and windshield cowl styles, these trucks are available for any type of body. Two additional Series give wide range of models for every need. See table for details.

1953 CHEVROLET, Carryall, Suburban, station wagon

1953 JAGUAR, Mark VII, 4-door sedan, automatic

Anywhere on earth...

Here on this barren stretch of the desolate "Skeleton Coast" in South West Africa, among rocky hills and dunes whipped into grotesque shapes by the corrosive blast of winds charged with salt and sand, diamonds are mined literally on the sea shore; and wherever men can work, so can the Land-Rover. A mobile or stationary power unit, a load or passenger-carrier, going anywhere... pulling anything, the 4-wheel drive Land-Rover can take it. All over the world, the Land-Rover stands for mobility, endurance, *toughness*.

...LAND-ROVER can take it

MADE BY THE ROVER COMPANY LIMITED · SOLIHULL · BIRMINGHAM also DEVONSHIRE HOUSE · LONDON

1953 LAND ROVER, Series 1, purchased used

1955 CHEVROLET, Nomad, station wagon

1955 MERCEDES BENZ, 220A, 4-door sedan

MERCEDES-BENZ 300-SL
Tomorrow's car —here today!

UPWARD OPENING DOORS are typical of design innovations for touring comfort and top sports performance in one great car.

DIRECT FUEL INJECTION, pioneered by Mercedes-Benz, gives you tremendous engine output, maximum power use, minimum gas consumption.

TO GIVE THE 300-SL its elegant aerodynamic styling the powerful 240 HP engine is mounted in a tilted position under the low, sleek hood.

No exhibition-hall dream, the 300-SL with its fabulous 240 hp fuel injection engine and dramatically functional body is here. At a snail's pace in city traffic up to 160 mph on the track, it creates tomorrow's standards of performance, handling ease, safety and comfort. Hand-finished details give the 300-SL traditional Mercedes-Benz elegance—in a car that breaks with all traditions.

You can see it today at any Mercedes-Benz showroom. You can drive it. You can own it—now!

Going to Europe? Choice of 8 Mercedes-Benz models delivered anywhere in Europe, from $2250

MERCEDES-BENZ
World's Oldest Makers of Automobiles

1956 MERCEDES BENZ, 300SL, 'Gull-Wing' sports car

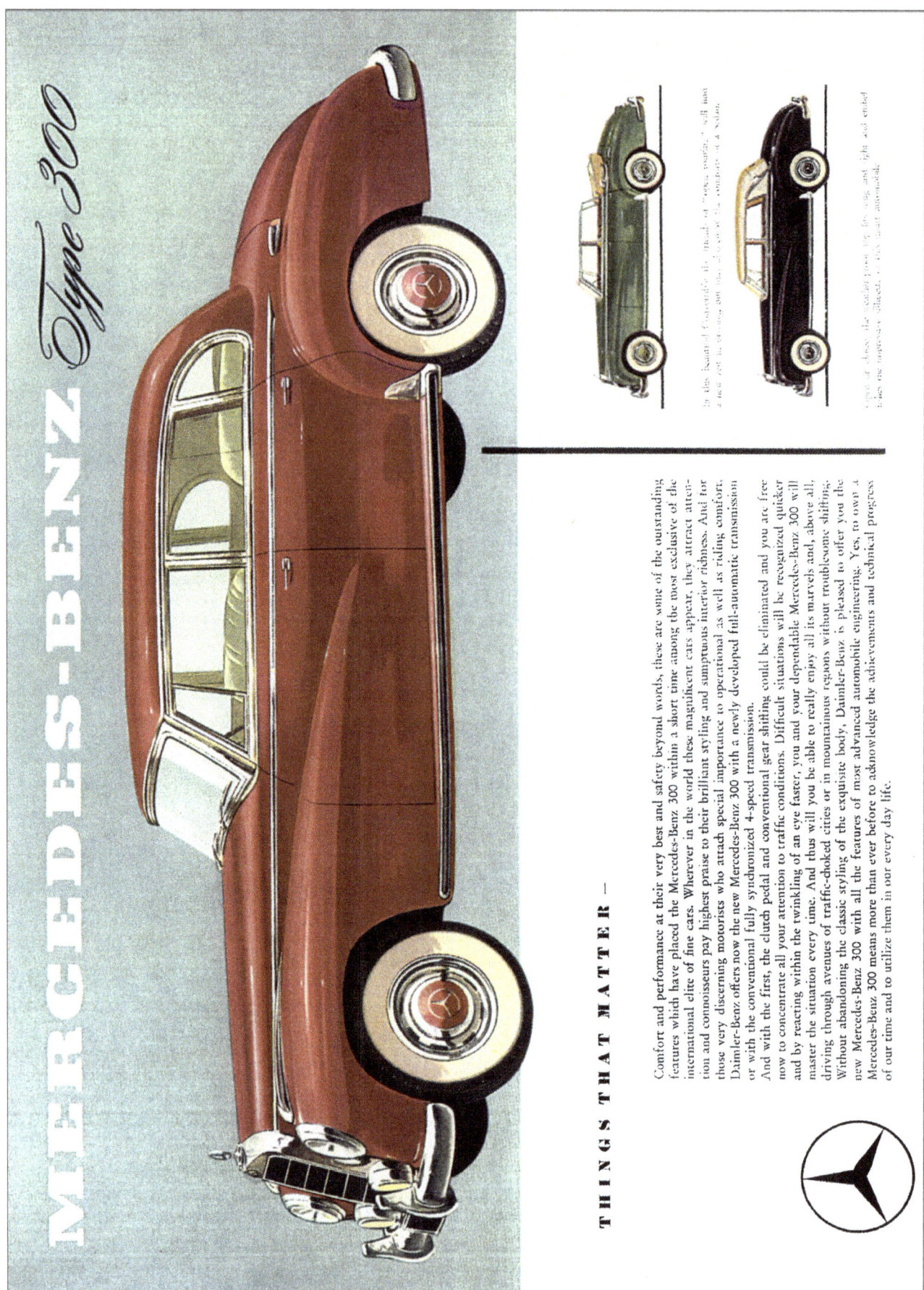

1956 MERCEDES BENZ, 300C, 4-door sedan

1956 PONTIAC, 4-door sedan

1956 VOLKSWAGEN, Beetle

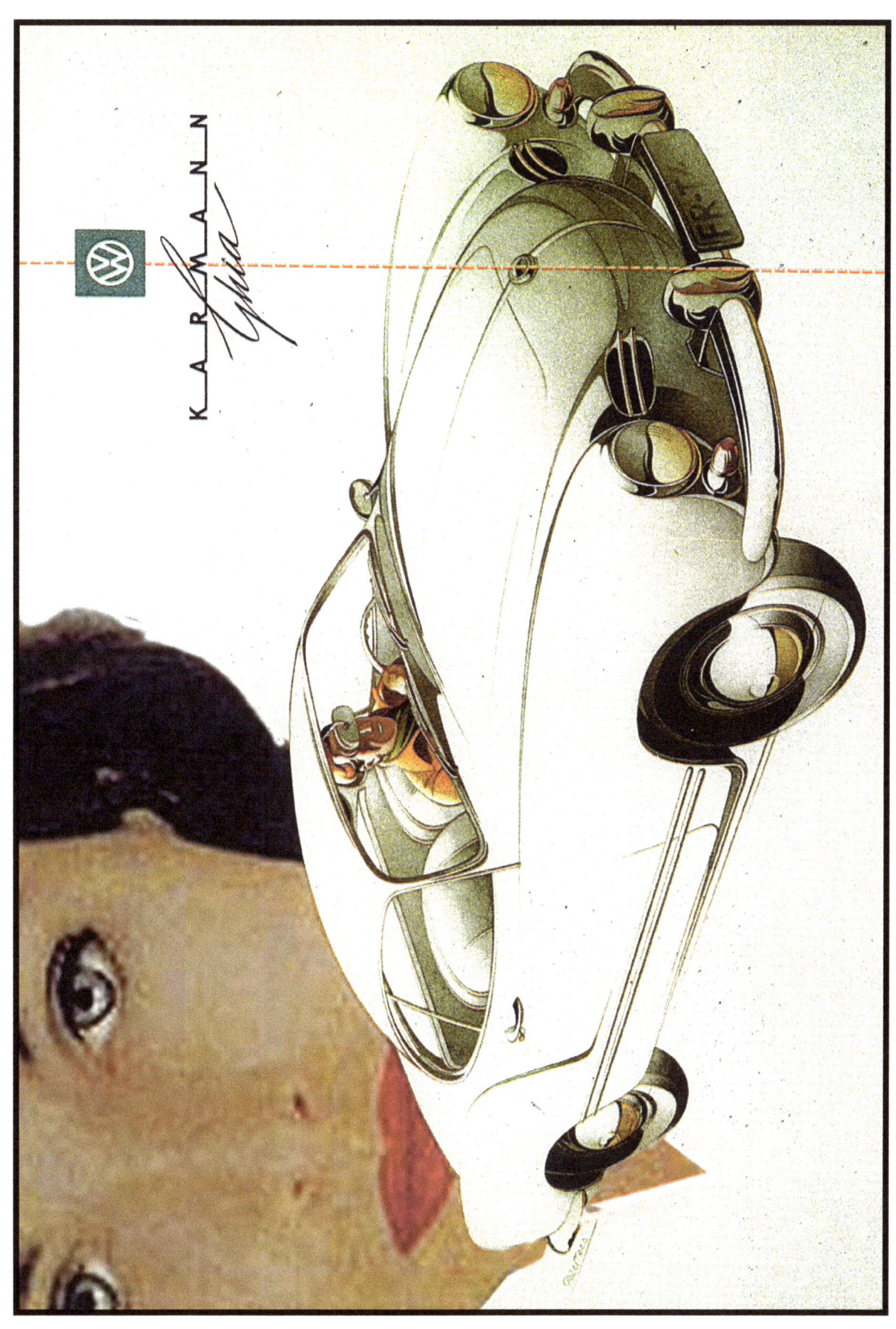

1956 VOLKSWAGEN, Karmann Ghia

Volkswagen Kombi

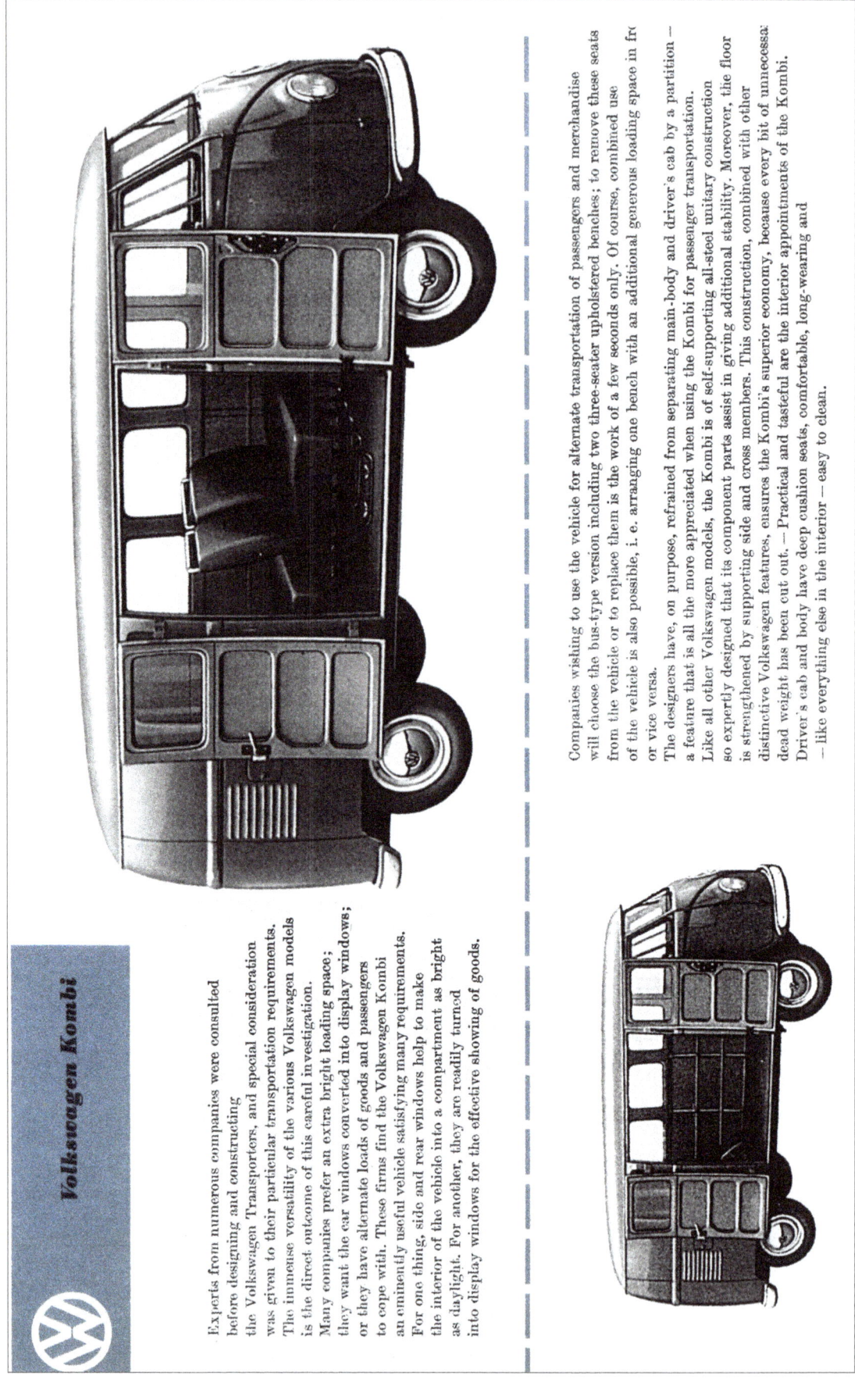

Experts from numerous companies were consulted before designing and constructing the Volkswagen Transporters, and special consideration was given to their particular transportation requirements. The immense versatility of the various Volkswagen models is the direct outcome of this careful investigation.

Many companies prefer an extra bright loading space; they want the car windows converted into display windows; or they have alternate loads of goods and passengers to cope with. These firms find the Volkswagen Kombi an eminently useful vehicle satisfying many requirements. For one thing, side and rear windows help to make the interior of the vehicle into a compartment as bright as daylight. For another, they are readily turned into display windows for the effective showing of goods.

Companies wishing to use the vehicle for alternate transportation of passengers and merchandise will choose the bus-type version including two three-seater upholstered benches; to remove these seats from the vehicle or to replace them is the work of a few seconds only. Of course, combined use of the vehicle is also possible, i. e. arranging one bench with an additional generous loading space in fr<!-- cut -->or vice versa.

The designers have, on purpose, refrained from separating main-body and driver's cab by a partition — a feature that is all the more appreciated when using the Kombi for passenger transportation. Like all other Volkswagen models, the Kombi is of self-supporting all-steel unitary construction so expertly designed that its component parts assist in giving additional stability. Moreover, the floor is strengthened by supporting side and cross members. This construction, combined with other distinctive Volkswagen features, ensures the Kombi's superior economy, because every bit of unnecessa<!-- cut -->dead weight has been cut out. — Practical and tasteful are the interior appointments of the Kombi. Driver's cab and body have deep cushion seats, comfortable, long-wearing and — like everything else in the interior — easy to clean.

1956 VOLKSWAGEN, Kombie

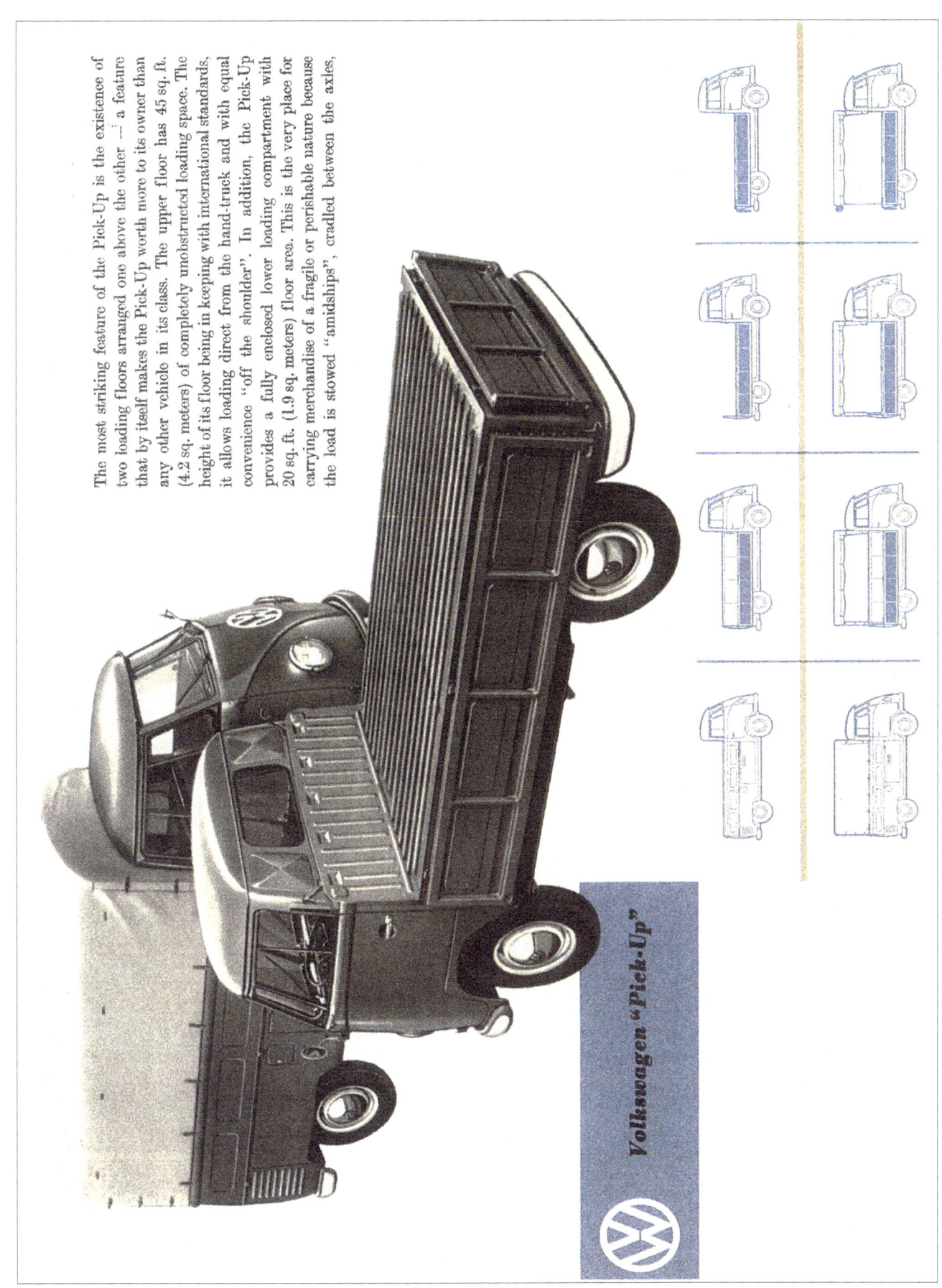

The most striking feature of the Pick-Up is the existence of two loading floors arranged one above the other — a feature that by itself makes the Pick-Up worth more to its owner than any other vehicle in its class. The upper floor has 45 sq. ft. (4.2 sq. meters) of completely unobstructed loading space. The height of its floor being in keeping with international standards, it allows loading direct from the hand-truck and with equal convenience "off the shoulder". In addition, the Pick-Up provides a fully enclosed lower loading compartment with 20 sq. ft. (1.9 sq. meters) floor area. This is the very place for carrying merchandise of a fragile or perishable nature because the load is stowed "amidships", cradled between the axles.

1956 VOLKSWAGEN, Pickup

Continental

In the great tradition of Rolls-Royce record-breaking is this 120 mile per hour luxury sports model. 1953 newly repainted tudor grey; upholstered in House of Lord's red leather; new whitewall tires; coachwork by H. J. Mulliner.
$12,500.

(New car in maroon with biscuit leather in stock at $19,699.)

Mark VI Sports Saloons

By far the largest number of Bentleys to enter the United States were Mark VI's produced, both body and chassis, at the Rolls-Royce factory. These bodies were so carefully designed that they have proved to be as desirable as custom bodies originally costing thousands more. Wide selection of lefthand drive models from $3750 to $7500. Many colors, automatic and manual transmission.

Sedanca Coupe ✓

One of the most beautiful Bentleys ever imported into the United States — coachwork by James Young. In this coupe body the metal portion over the driver's seat slides back entirely into the roof. A 1953 model in silver with tangerine upholstery. Condition superior.
$8500.

1958 — 1953 BENTLEY, James Young, Sedanca, purchased used

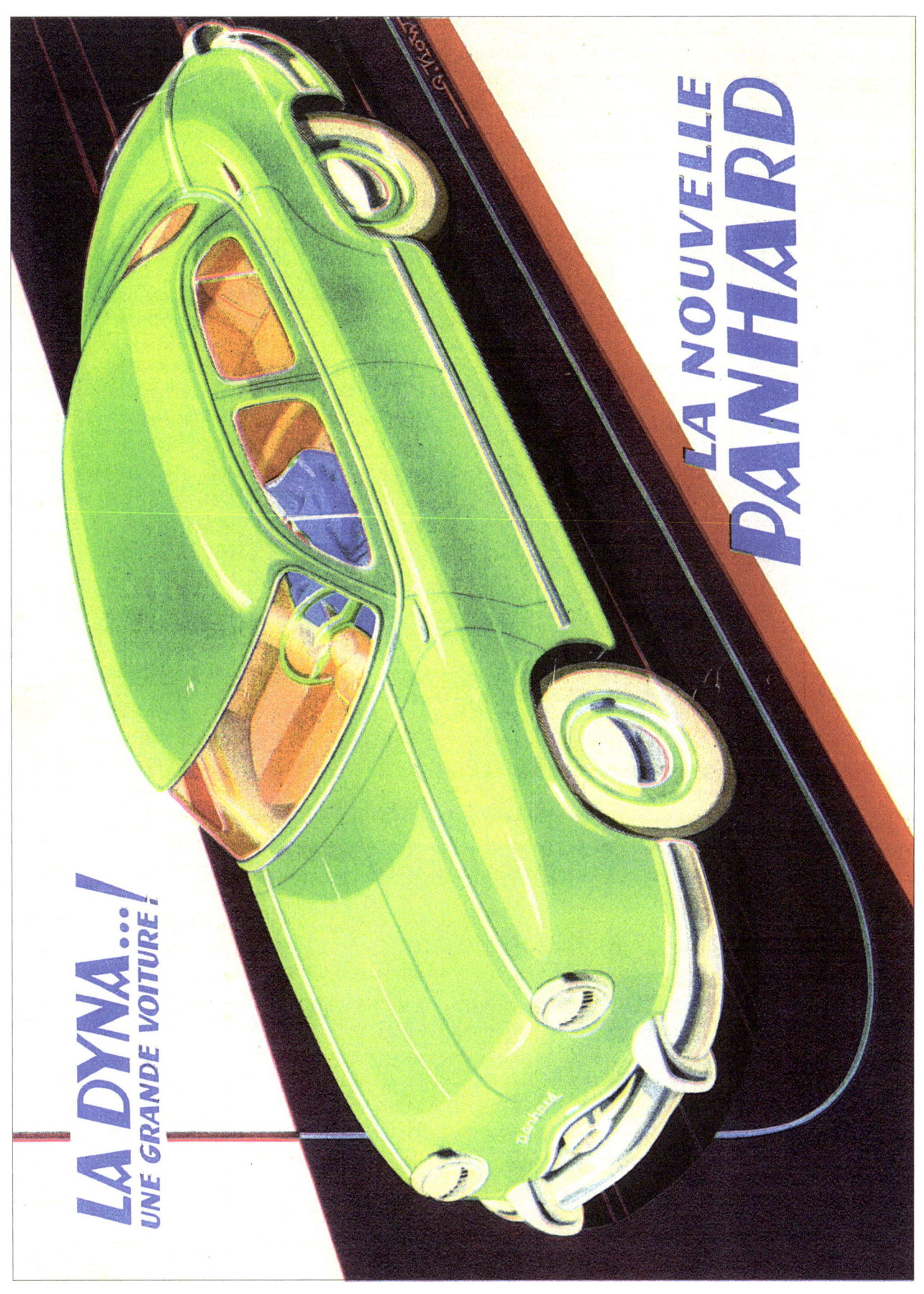

1958 PANHARD, Dyna, 4-door sedan

FURY V-800—Specifications

Advanced design 8-cylinder V-type. Horsepower 290 at 5400 RPM. Torque 325 ft./lbs. at 4000 RPM. Compression ratio 9.25:1. Bore 3.91 inches. Stroke 3.31 inches. Piston displacement 318 cubic inches. New design 8-barrel carburetion system with balanced fuel flow to each cylinder and separate idle air bleed inlets. Matching intake manifold. Two special offset design dry paper replaceable element air cleaners. Over-head valves. Adjustable valve tappets. High-load valve springs. Pistons especially designed for high-compression ratio. Special high-performance camshaft. Special high-performance resistor-type spark plugs. Automatic mechanical and vacuum spark control. New splash-proof dual-breaker distributor. New spool-type rubber shear engine mounts. Vibration damper. Rotary-type oil pump. Shunt-type oil filter. Oil capacity 5 quarts. Full-pressure lubrication to all crankshaft, camshaft, and connecting rod bearings and to valve rocker arms and tappets. Special low-restriction dual-exhaust system.

SPECIAL HIGH-PERFORMANCE CHASSIS

A special high-performance chassis is standard with every Fury V-800 installation. This includes heavy-duty torsion-bar springs and ball joints, heavy-duty Oriflow shock absorbers both front and rear, and heavy-duty 2½-inch rear springs. Special 14 x 6 inch Safety-Rim wheels and 7.50 x 14 tires are also supplied at no extra cost.

TRANSMISSION OPTIONS

The fiery new Fury V-800 engine may be teamed with either Plymouth's 3-speed manual Synchro-Silent transmission, or 3-speed fully automatic TorqueFlite Push-Button transmission at moderate extra cost. Rear-axle ratio is 3.73:1 with manual, 3.36:1 with TorqueFlite. Other axle ratios available on special order.

The V-800 engine is standard on the Fury (above), and available at moderate cost on all other Plymouth models!

1958 PLYMOUTH, Fury, apprentices' gift to Olgivanna

1958 SEARS, Lectracar, golf cart, gift from H. Price

PERFECT REFLECTION
of your very particular taste

Name your favorite color—the Star Chief has it, in 13 smart, easy-to-get-along-with shades of long-lasting acrylic lacquer finish and nine two-tone cloth and four coated-fabric interiors. Even the carpeting takes on distinction with tiny flecks of silver or gold imbedded in the deep pile . . . and the easily washable headlining is dotted with tiny stars to add glamour to every action-packed mile you drive.

STAR CHIEF SEDAN

1959 PONTIAC, 4 door sedan, purchased for Iovanna

FINAL INVENTORY OF FRANK LLOYD WRIGHT FOUNDATION CARS

The following is a list, in alphabetical order, of the cars that the Frank Lloyd Wright Foundation owned when Wright passed away in 1959:

1937 AC, Ace, sports car

1952 Austin, A40, sedan

1953 Bentley, Sedanca, custom designed cabriolet

1952 Crosley, Hot Shot (2), convertible

1953 Chevrolet, Suburban, station wagon

1955 Chevrolet, Nomad, station wagon

1929 Cord Cabriolet

1951 Crosley, Farm-a-Road, tractor

1953 Ford, Ranch Wagon, station wagon

1953 Ford, Country Squire, station wagon

1952 Hillman, convertible

1948 Jaguar, Mark IV, convertible

1949 Jaguar, Mark V, sedan

1953 Jaguar, Mark VII, sedan

1940 Lincoln Continental, modified convertible

1941 Lincoln Continental, sedan

1956 Mercedes Benz, 300C, sedan

1956 Mercedes Benz, 300SL, sports car

1958 Panhard, Dyna, sedan

1956 Pontiac, sedan

1959 Pontiac, sedan

1951 Riley, sedan

1956 VW, sedan

1956 VW, Karmann Ghia

1956 VW, Kombie

1956 VW, pickup

1958 Sears, Lectracar, golf cart

Note: There are a total of 29 cars listed. They include 15 different makes, plus one Sears golf cart. As of September 2012, only the following Wright cars were known to still exist: the AC Ace, the Bentley, the Cord, the two Lincoln Continentals, the Mercedes Benz 300SL, and a Crosley Hot Shot that was assembled from parts taken off wrecked Wright-owned Crosleys that were no longer operational.

WRIGHT'S TWO CAR-RELATED PROJECTS

Mercedes-Benz showroom designed by Frank Lloyd Wright, formerly a Jaguar showroom, New York City (1954).

1956 Lindholm Phillips 66 gas station designed by Frank Lloyd Wright.

ACKNOWLEDGEMENTS

Given the scant literature that exists about Wright and his cars, uncovering the full extent of his lifelong involvement with the automobile proved to be a daunting task. This publication brought to light one of Wright's great passions — the automobile. It was done with the aid of a significant number of people, especially those listed below.

Mary Jane Hamilton, author and Wright scholar, played the most important role in making this book happen. She was my guide, mentor, role model, sounding board, cheerleader, consultant, and inspiration throughout this entire multi-year project.

Casie Kesterson, a Getty approved researcher, did my research. I could not have found a better researcher anywhere for this project.

Other people who have helped me create this catalog of Wright Foundation owned cars include: Arnold Roy, Indira Berndtson, Thomas Heinz, Jennifer Helm, Anna Golomb, Anna Barnhill Reichert, Ron Kimball, Robin Surface, Jim Bollman, Pedro Guerrero, Laura Helsher, Kim Miller, Eric Wright, John Hess, Brandoch Peters, Joe Fabris, Pat Thym, Bill Schroeder, Gary Klein, Bob and Cathy Cunningham, John Ottenheimer, Michael Dingman, Scott McNair, Dixie Leger, Suzette Lucas, Barbara Thompson, Ed Winkler, Andrew Morland, Jon Bill, Bob Horning, Bob Van Zant, Tom Sherry, Pete Dottl, Paul Richard, William Stoessel, Richard Earl, Noel Ruessmann, and others.

I would also like to acknowledge Sigmund Freud's observation that "sometimes a cigar is just a cigar." In my opinion, it also applies to Wright's passion for cars. Sometimes a car buff is just a car buff and one should not attach any psychological significance of the design features of his choice of cars to his work.

Like most of Frank Lloyd Wright's cars, this 1952 Austin ended up in a junkyard.

www.ingramcontent.com/pod-product-compliance
Lightning Source LLC
Chambersburg PA
CBHW061127070526
44584CB00033B/4245